# Between You & Me...

## Titles in the Seedbed Daily Text series:

*Listen to Him: Luke* by J. D. Walt
*(un)Puzzled: Ephesians* by J. D. Walt
*The Domino Effect: Colossians* by J. D. Walt
*The First Real Christian: James* by J. D. Walt
*This Is How We Know: 1 John* by J. D. Walt
*Between You and Me: 2 John, 3 John, Philemon,*
    *Titus, and Jude* by Omar Rikabi
*Right Here, Right Now, Jesus: Prayer* by J. D. Walt
*The Advent Mission: Advent* by Omar Rikabi
*Protagonist: Advent* by Matt LeRoy and Josh LeRoy
*Reset: Advent* by J. D. Walt

he
eedbed
aily Text

# Between You & Me...

ı 3 John, Philemon
us, Jude

MAR RIKABI

Printed in the United States of America

*Cover and page design by Strange Last Name*
*Page layout by PerfecType, Nashville, Tennessee*

**Rikabi, Omar.**
  Between you and & me : 2 & 3 John, Philemon, Titus, Jude / Omar Rikabi. – Franklin, Tennessee : Seedbed Publishing, ©2019.

    pages ;  cm.  (The Seedbed daily text)

    ISBN 9781628247435 (paperback)
    ISBN 9781628247442 (Mobi)
    ISBN 9781628247503 (ePub)
    ISBN 9781628247510 (uPDF)


    1. Bible. Epistles--Meditations.  2. Bible. Epistles of John--Meditations.
    3. Bible. Philemon--Meditations.  4. Bible. Titus--Meditations.  5. Bible.
    Jude--Meditations.  I. Title. II. Between you and me. III. Seedbed daily text.

BS2635.4.R54 2019                          242.5                    2019955215

SEEDBED PUBLISHING
Franklin, Tennessee
seedbed.com

For Granny and PaPa

# Contents

# How the Daily Text Works

You may not know this, but the Daily Text is written, well, daily by J. D. Walt, myself, and some other friends. Our inside joke for it is "making the donuts" because they're written fresh daily, then posted online and recorded for a podcast for the next day (and if you haven't already, you can subscribe to receive the daily e-mail at dailytext.seedbed.com).

You may have an image J. D. or me writing well ahead of schedule in a quiet, mahogany-paneled study or a well-lit recording studio, but that's way off. J. D. has a chair he usually writes in, but if you listen carefully to the recordings you sometimes can hear his kids getting breakfast in the background. I usually write in our bedroom closet. And, many times, the Daily Text has been written and recorded in the backseat of cars, restaurants, hotels, and even once (full disclosure) an airport family bathroom.

While sometimes "making the donuts" is done playfully, we do not take this work lightly. While we do prayerfully map out where we think it's going in advance, the Daily Text is literally map-making. We know where it'll end, but we're not sure from day to day what it'll look like getting there. We usually begin with the prayer, "Lord, give me a word today" because this is truly an exercise in faith and the work of the Holy Spirit.

The hardest part for me of writing the Daily Text is the daily limit. There is only so much that can be said of each text per day. These are not exhaustive, theological treatises, but daily devotionals for prayer and discipleship. This book is the culmination of some of those devotions.

The goal of Scripture and the Daily Text is not just information, but a transformation that leads to action. While Scripture always addresses us personally, it is not written to us individually. The content of Scripture cries out for a community to address, and the Daily Text is made for discipleship in community. And keep in mind, the Daily Text is not called the Daily Text for kicks. We believe Scripture is worthy of our most focused and consistent attention. Every day. We all have misses, but let's make every day more than a noble aspiration. Let's make it our covenant with one another.

Here is a suggested plan for using the Daily Text as a resource for a small group or class setting:

### *Band Together*

Gather your group and set apart your time together, maybe with the saying of the Lord's Prayer or the lighting of a candle. Give each person an opportunity to check in with what is happening in their life since you last met. Ask the question: How is it with your soul? Or, How is your life with God?

### *Pray*

Take a few moments to intentionally pray for each other. Also pray for your church, for your city, even for the events in the world you see on the news. Ask the Holy Spirit to open the eyes of your hearts to see Jesus during your time together.

## Listen

The living Word of God is the primary text here. Invite the group to settle into silence for a period of no less than one and no more than five minutes. Ask an appointed person to keep time and then to read each of the Scripture passages covering the period of days since the last group meeting. Allow at least one minute of silence following the reading of the Scriptures.

## Respond

Invite anyone from the group to respond to the hearing of Scripture by answering these prompts: What did you hear? What did you see? What did you otherwise sense from the Lord?

## Share

Moving in an orderly rotation (or free-for-all), invite people to share reflections and implications for discipleship from the week's readings. For the first gathering, it could be helpful to have each person answer the question, What are your expectations?

Allow group conversation to proceed at will. Limit to one sharing item per turn with multiple rounds of discussion.

## Go

Invite each person to share a single discipleship or mission intention for the week ahead. At each person's turn, he or she is invited to share how their intention went during the previous week. The class or group can close their meeting according to their established patterns or create a new one.

# Introduction: An Open Letter

I wrote my first letter at five years old. Actually, I dictated it to my mom. My friend next door was mean and didn't want to play with me anymore. My feelings were hurt and I wanted to share my hurt with someone special: my grandfather, PaPa.

Through tears and sniffles I told the whole story and how I was sad and how I really, really, really wished I could be with my PaPa on his farm and I couldn't wait to see him again. Then we sealed it up and mailed it the next day. A couple of weeks later, I got his letter back saying how sorry he was and that he couldn't wait to see me too.

My grandmother took a picture of him sitting in front of the garage reading my letter with his favorite rat terrier, Little Bit, sitting in his lap. He has a deep smile on his face as he reads, the kind of smile that exists when a PaPa and his grandson are best friends. It's a picture I still have sitting above my desk as I write this.

Although my mom was my scribe, my letter was personal. I only wanted it to be between him and me, but, of course, now I've shared it with you. And that's the nature of some letters in the New Testament: 2 and 3 John, Philemon, Titus, Jude . . . these letters are some of the letters written to individuals or to churches so small they met around the dinner table in someone's house.

And they're short. Some are not even a full chapter—just a few verses—and others aren't much more. These letters are not sermons, but instead share an intimacy, like that between best friends. The kind of intimacy that could begin with "this is just between you and me," because they write about specific people and specific situations; not the kind of stuff you broadcast to everyone.

Writers like John probably didn't expect these little letters to end up in the canon of Scripture for millions to read over the next two thousand years, but here they are. That these personal notes ended up in the Bible tells us that our personal relationships—the things "between you and me"— can have an impact beyond us, influencing people and places for generations to come, even for eternity.

The folks that wrote and read these little letters were people who believed that Jesus Christ had lived, died, lived again, gone to sit at God's right hand, sent the Holy Spirit, and would come back again in final victory. Which puts them in the same part of the story as us: a Pentecost people waiting for Jesus to return. And, until then, they dealt with a lot of the same basic stuff we deal with today: the joys and struggles over who Jesus is and who his followers are to be with each other.

We're going to look at a few of these scriptural postcards—the ones so small they never get their own Bible study or sermon series—to see how things can be made and kept holy between you and me.

For the awakening,

Omar Al-Rikabi
Abbey of Gethsemani
Pentecost 2019

Between You & Me...

# The Truth about Truth

**2 JOHN 1–2** | This letter is from John, the elder.

I am writing to the chosen lady and to her children, whom I love in the truth—as does everyone else who knows the truth—because the truth lives in us and will be with us forever.

### Consider This

"Daddy, you're not the boss of me," my then five-year-old daughter said after I warned her of a consequence for not finishing dinner. Then her seven-year-old big sister beat me to a response: "Yes he is! God says our parents are the bosses of us to love us and take care of us!"

I knew that big sister was learning about the Ten Commandments in Sunday school, so I turned to my (now favored) child to say, "That's right! Where does God say that?" But before I could, little sister shot back, "Well, God says I'm the boss of me."

Big sister and I stared at little sister, but she didn't look up from her plate. "Where did God say you're the boss of you?" I slowly asked, breaking the silence. Looking out the window she said, "Ummmm . . . he said so in my heart." Chagrined, I walked out of the kitchen and handed her over to her mother.

We are in the era of "live your truth," and it starts at a very young age. "Your truth" is what you feel or experience. Whatever is true for you is good, and whatever is true for me is good.[1] But what is truth? *To be true* means "to be in accordance with reality." But what if we each have a different reality, and what does John mean when he says the truth lives in us?

In his much larger gospel account, John records Jesus' conversation during his last meal before his crucifixion. In John 14:6 Jesus says, "I am the way, *the truth*, and the life. No one can come to the Father except through me" (emphasis added). The Greek word John uses in his gospel for Jesus as the "truth" (*alēthela*) is the same word he uses here in his letter. In other words, truth is not a concept or a series of propositions or even personal experience. Truth is a Person. Our experiences and feelings, though legitimate and important, are subjective. But Jesus Christ is constant. He is our reality.

This is not an easy thing to grasp or live into. It's why we need grace. And prevenient grace—the grace of God that is pursuing all people even if they're not aware of it—means that whenever someone is looking for absolute truth, what they're really looking for is Jesus, even if they're not aware of it. (Pro tip: this is where to pray and intercede between you and others.)

So here's a good place to start: John's statement that the truth will "be with us forever" is the same Greek word he uses in his gospel during that same meal when Jesus says,

---

1. After I wrote this entry, my friend David Drury tweeted it better than I could say: "'My truth,' which is somewhat meaningless, should be [replaced] in all speech with 'my story' which is always meaningful—and I suspect that is what people really mean when they want to be heard. My story is made up of truth—my truth can easily be made up of lies."

"Remain in me, and I will remain in you. For a branch cannot produce fruit if it is severed from the vine, and you cannot be fruitful unless you remain in me" (John 15:4).

A friend once taught me the practice of a *breath prayer*: In silence, as you breath in deep, let your prayer be, "Jesus remain in me." And as you breathe out slowly, let your prayer be, "and I will remain in you."

Pray it now. Then pray it again as you breathe again. Pray it throughout the day. Pray it for several days. For weeks. You can pray it anytime and anywhere you take a breath. Let it become your truth—as close and true as the air you breathe—so that the things between you and Christ can impact the things between you and me.

### The Prayer

Jesus, remain in me . . . and I will remain in you. Amen.

### The Question

- What has been your truth?

# The Truth about Fathers and Sons

2

**2 JOHN 3–4 NIV** | Grace, mercy and peace from God the Father and from Jesus Christ, the Father's Son, will be with us in truth and love.

It has given me great joy to find some of your children walking in the truth, just as the Father commanded us.

### Consider This

I was preaching the prodigal son story in Luke 15 to a group of college students, the one N. T. Wright says should really be called the Running Father story, because it's really about God's steadfast love for us no matter what.[2] There was one girl who was just not having it. I could see in her eyes that she didn't want to hear about God as a loving, caring Father who runs to his rebellious kids. And in what could only be a Holy Spirit–inspired moment, I suddenly went off script and blurted out, "This story sounds great unless you had a terrible father."

At that moment tears came to her eyes, and I realized something I had never given much thought to before: a child forms their primary ideas of God from how they are parented. Many of us struggle with Jesus teaching us to pray by first calling God "Our Daddy."

Some of us had wonderful relationships with our fathers and can see God as caring, safe, and loving. But because of our experiences, for many of us to think of God as a father causes us to see him as distant, angry, abandoning, or even abusive.

As two of my friends wrote, the ache is there because deep down inside we know what a good father should be like.[3]

---

2. N. T. Wright, *The Lord and His Prayer* (Grand Rapids, MI: William B. Eerdmans Publishing, 1996), 50.
3. Matt LeRoy and Jeremy Summers, *Awakening Grace: Spiritual Practices That Transform Your Soul* (Indianapolis, IN: Wesleyan Publishing House, 2012), 54.

What many tend to do is throw out this image and language of God as Father altogether. But if grace, mercy, and peace come to us between a Father and Son relationship, what do we do?

We look to the truth . . . we look at Jesus. When we see the nature of Jesus, we see the nature of the heavenly Father. In Matthew 7:11 Jesus says, "So if you sinful people know how to give good gifts to your children, how much more will your heavenly Father give good gifts to those who ask him."

The key phrase is "how much more." How much more perfect is the heavenly Father than any of our earthly fathers could ever be? We pray "your kingdom come"; even though world history is full of violent and oppressive kingdoms and leaders, we still pray to embrace God's rule as a kingdom because of how much more perfect it is being made on earth as it is heaven through Jesus Christ.

I suspect that many of us are somewhere in between embrace and ache because our fathers loved us, but also operated out of their own sin and wounds. So the best we can hope for is the way Ron Reagan described his relationship with his father, the fortieth president of the United States: "We all grow up idolizing, [then] dethroning, and with luck, later befriending our fathers, but can we really know them? Do they care to know us?"[4]

Look at how Jesus describes the relationship in *The Message* translation of Matthew 11:27: "The Father has given

---

4. Ron Reagan "My Father, the President," *Parade*, January 16, 2011, www.parade .com/116131/ronreagan/16-my-father-the-president.

me all these things to do and say. This is a unique Father-Son operation, coming out of Father and Son intimacies and knowledge. No one knows the Son the way the Father does, nor the Father the way the Son does. But I'm not keeping it to myself; I'm ready to go over it line by line with anyone willing to listen."

There is grace, mercy, and peace found here between the Father and the Son—the kind that can heal the ache and longing we've had for the daddy or mommy we've always wanted and change things between all of us.

### The Prayer

Jesus, remain in me and I will remain in you. Please show me in a real way how the love between you and me comes from the love between you and the heavenly Father. Amen.

### The Question

- Has seeing God as Father been a blessing or a curse and how might Jesus heal that image?

# 3 The Truth about Love

**2 JOHN 5–6** | I am writing to remind you, dear friends, that we should love one another. This is not a new commandment, but one we have had from the beginning. Love means doing what God has commanded us, and he has commanded us to love one another, just as you heard from the beginning.

### Consider This

Love.

As Inigo Montoya says in *The Princess Bride*, "You keep using that word. I do not think it means what you think it means."

Webster's defines *love* as "strong affection for another" or an "attraction based on sexual desires."

Now I can have strong affections for, say, *Star Wars* or the Dallas Cowboys, but is that true love? And I can be sexually attracted to my wife, but I can also find someone else attractive. Does that mean I truly love another person in the context of my marriage vows?

I'm going with no. Feelings come and go. They're circumstantial. And they're ultimately about what I want or desire. So if Jesus is the truth, and he gave us the command to love one another, then what is the truth about love?

When it was getting close to his crucifixion, a religious expert tried to trap Jesus by asking,

> "Teacher, which is the most important commandment in the law of Moses?" Jesus replied, "'You must love the LORD your God with all your heart, all your soul, and all your mind.' This is the first and greatest commandment. A second is equally important: 'Love your neighbor as yourself.' The entire law and all the demands of the prophets are based on these two commandments." (Matt. 22:36–40)

But what if that's not enough? What if loving others as I love myself is incomplete or problematic between you and me? Because what if I'm an introvert, and to love others as I love myself means to be left alone? What if I'm a narcissist? Or if my love language is significant touch and quality time and yours is gifts and time alone? What if my attitude is "Jesus loves you, but the rest of us think you're a jerk"? Or I'm wounded and the best I can do is "Jesus loves you, I don't have to"?

All this to say, what if I'm loving myself out of my own truth instead of the truth of Jesus Christ?

This is why Jesus gives a new command, something above and beyond loving others as we love ourselves. A new command that doesn't replace the law of Moses, but completes it. It's in John's Gospel when Jesus is washing his disciples' feet and serving them dinner right before his crucifixion. He says, "So now I am giving you a new commandment: Love each other. Just as I have loved you, you should love each other" (John 13:34).

Just as I have loved you.

When I love you like I love myself, it can be about feelings.

When I love you like Jesus loved us, it is a crucifixion choice.

When I love myself, it's too often about holding on to my desires, rights, and entitlements. When I love as Jesus loved me, it's giving up my desires, rights, and entitlements.

It's what J. D. Walt has called over and over in the Daily Text "the second half of the gospel." The first half is John 3:16: "For this is how God loved the world: He gave his one and only Son, so that everyone who believes in him will not perish but have eternal life."

The second half is 1 John 3:16: "We know what real love is because Jesus gave up his life for us. So we also ought to give up our lives for our brothers and sisters."

And as the saying goes, the world will see the first half of the gospel when we embrace the second half. That's how it works between you and me.

In 2 John he is reminding us of the truth about love. And we need the reminder because as we're about to see in the second half of his letter, true love does not always mean what we think it means.

### The Prayer

Jesus, remain in me and I will remain in you. I can love like you because you loved me first. Bit by bit, keep changing me from loving like myself to loving like you. Amen.

### The Question

- What's love got to do with it?

# The Truth about What We Believe

4

2 JOHN 7–9  |  I say this because many deceivers have gone out into the world. They deny that Jesus Christ came in a real body. Such a person is a deceiver and an antichrist. Watch out that you do not lose what we have worked so hard to achieve.

Be diligent so that you receive your full reward. Anyone who wanders away from this teaching has no relationship with God. But anyone who remains in the teaching of Christ has a relationship with both the Father and the Son.

### *Consider This*

My daughters are required to start each school day reciting the Pledge of Allegiance (but we live in Texas, which means they're also required to say the Pledge of Allegiance to the Flag of Texas. Given the way pledges work, I think it means they cancel out each other—but I'm no expert).

They do this for the same reason the National Anthem is sung before sporting events: pledges and anthems declare the story of who a people are and what they hold most sacred. They confer identity on a people group because their declarations are considered non-negotiable.

Which is why every Sunday at the church I pastor we open the service with everyone standing and saying the Apostles' Creed:

> I believe in God, the Father Almighty,
> creator of heaven and earth.
> I believe in Jesus Christ, his only Son, our Lord,
> who was conceived by the Holy Spirit,
> born of the Virgin Mary,
> suffered under Pontius Pilate,
> was crucified, died, and was buried;
> he descended to the dead.

On the third day he rose again;
he ascended into heaven,
is seated at the right hand of the Father,
and will come again to judge the living and the dead.
I believe in the Holy Spirit,
the holy catholic [universal] church,
the communion of saints,
the forgiveness of sins,
the resurrection of the body,
and the life everlasting. Amen.

This creed is the ancient pledge and anthem of our faith. It is the non-negotiable of what it means to be Christian. Denominations have their dogma (like free will vs. predestination) and then there are opinions (like liturgical vs. modern worship). But regardless of dogma or opinion, doctrine matters. The Apostles' Creed matters. It is non-negotiable.

The first believers dealt with this stuff too. Like when they argued if someone needed circumcision to be saved or if it was okay for a believer to eat food that had been offered in worship to idols. But what was not up for debate was the very basics of the faith: Jesus is the only way to the Father. He is the Son of God who came to earth in a real body, through a virgin birth, who died for our sins and then rose from the dead, then went to heaven and is coming back again.

If we can't hold to these basics, then is our belief really Christian?

At least that is what John is saying in today's text. It seems there were folks in the church he's writing to that denied a non-negotiable: Jesus existed in a real body, which is the most basic of basic Christian doctrine.

He calls them deceivers, which Webster's defines as "to make someone believe something that is not true." And given what we've already seen in this letter about what truth is, John is saying there are folks in the church who are moving others away from Jesus to their own truth. He calls them an anti-Christ, not in a derogatory way, but factually because what they are preaching and doing is opposed to the basic truth of who Christ is and our identity in their relationship as Father and Son.

This is a warning for believers across all time and all places, because if John is writing about this issue back then to a few friends and this little letter made it into the canon of Holy Scripture, it seems it can still be an issue today between you and me.

### The Prayer

Jesus, abide in me and I will abide in you. Help me know the truth about who you are and may that truth set me free. Amen.

### The Question

- What is your non-negotiable in the faith and is it a matter of doctrine, dogma, or opinion?

# The Truth about the Church

# 5

2 JOHN 10–13 NIV | If anyone comes to you and does not bring this teaching, do not take them into your house or welcome them. Anyone who welcomes them shares in their wicked work.

I have much to write to you, but I do not want to use paper and ink. Instead, I hope to visit you and talk with you face to face, so that our joy may be complete.

The children of your sister, who is chosen by God, send their greetings.

### Consider This

I thought Jesus said the church is supposed to love everyone? Aren't we supposed to welcome all people—"come as you are" and all that? But now here is John saying don't invite people into your home who believe different than you.

Except that isn't what he's saying.

But first a little background on the kind of church John is writing to. These earliest churches would meet in a person's home. These were intimate gatherings, usually with a meal, that could fit in a small room. We're talking just a few people. No announcements; no turn and greet your neighbor; no "Do we have any visitors with us this morning?" Just a few people meeting to pray and talk about Jesus together.

There was also a strong cultural practice of welcoming and showing hospitality to strangers and traveling teachers. It was understood that you welcomed them as though they were Christ. And it is these very teachers that John is talking about. Did you catch it? "If anyone comes to your meeting and *does not teach the truth about Christ*" (v. 10, emphasis added).

These are the folks he's already called deceivers; the ones he said were teaching the incarnation of Jesus wasn't real. And he's already called these teachers anti-Christ, so there's no welcoming them as Christ.

Is this harsh? Sounds like it in our current "live your truth" culture, but we must also remember that the early church followed the scriptural guidelines for removing people from the congregation for sin, something many of us would bristle at today (see Matthew 18:15–17).

With a passage like this, there is a difference between welcoming an unbeliever and welcoming someone who is intentionally leading people to unbelief. John is talking about those who come into an intimate setting built on the relationship between the Father and the Son and intentionally try to teach something else. This is where love is tough because love also protects (see 1 Corinthians 13:7).

The tough love John's talking about here is to protect us from our faith becoming aimless. Remember in yesterday's text John wrote: "Anyone who wanders away from this teaching has no relationship with God" (2 John 9).

And what is the opposite of wandering away? To remain: "But anyone who remains in the teaching of Christ has a relationship with both the Father and the Son" (v. 9b).

As we saw at the beginning, this is the same word Jesus uses in John 15:4 saying, "Remain in me, and I will remain in you."

This is also a warning for today, because we don't just suddenly walk away from the faith and abiding in Jesus Christ. Wandering is lazy. It takes time. You may not even know you're getting lost until it's too late. So remain in the truth. That is the heart of the message between John and his friends, and between you and me.

### The Prayer

Jesus, remain in me and I will remain in you. Amen.

### The Question

- What warning do you hear today?

# What Twitter Teaches Us about the Word of God

# 6

3 JOHN 1–4 | This letter is from John, the elder.

I am writing to Gaius, my dear friend, whom I love in the truth.

Dear friend, I hope all is well with you and that you are as healthy in body as you are strong in spirit. Some of the traveling teachers recently returned and made me very happy by telling me about your faithfulness and that you are living according to the truth. I could have no greater joy than to hear that my children are following the truth.

### Consider This

John's third letter is the shortest book in all the Bible. At just fifteen verses, it's the Twitter post of Scripture. Let's start with "I am writing to Gaius, my dear friend." It's a short message to an old friend, and I'm pretty sure John never imagined it would go viral. But here it is in the canon of Holy Scripture. There's a lesson here we should consider before we dig into what John wants to get across. What's the lesson? That everything we say matters.

Everything.

Consider what the Scriptures say about words:

- Genesis 1:3ff: "Then God said, 'Let there be . . . ,' and there was . . ."
- Ezekiel 3:1: The voice said to me, "Son of man, eat what I am giving you—eat this scroll! Then go and give its message to the people of Israel."
- Revelation 1:19: "Write down what you have seen—both the things that are now happening and the things that will happen."
- Proverbs 18:21: "The tongue can bring death or life; those who love to talk will reap the consequences."

- James 3:9–10 (NIV): "With the tongue we praise our Lord and Father, and with it we curse human beings, who have been made in God's likeness. Out of the same mouth come praise and cursing."

In other words, every word matters. Most of what we say, write, post, text, or tweet has the power to speak truth or lies. To create life or death—into our lives and the lives of others. We live in a time with so many throwaway comments (in person and online) that have the power to destroy or build up, to bring a blessing or a curse.

A single tweet is 280 characters that can be read by no one, or it can start a riot. John's letter is fifteen verses that started as a personal note and now is part of the Word of God. Like John's little letter he intended only for his friend, you never know who's ultimately going to read or hear what you have to say, and how God wants to use it as a word of good news.

### The Prayer

Heavenly Father, may the words of my mouth and the thoughts of my heart be pleasing to you. Let what I say hold the power of your salvation. In Jesus' name, amen.

### The Question

- How can the ideas in today's text help transform how you communicate?

# 7 Dealing with Stranger Things

3 JOHN 5–8 NIV  |  Dear friend, you are faithful in what you are doing for the brothers and sisters, even though they are strangers to you. They have told the church about your love. Please send them on their way in a manner that honors God. It was for the sake of the Name that they went out, receiving no help from the pagans. We ought therefore to show hospitality to such people so that we may work together for the truth.

### Consider This

There is a Trappist monastery in Bardstown, Kentucky, called The Abbey of Our Lady of Gethsemani. You can go there for a silent retreat and pray with the monks, and as you enter the guest house the rule of St. Benedict is carved into the wall. It reads: "Let all guests who come be received like Christ."

I think it has a double meaning. First, receive any guest as you would if Jesus in the flesh were coming over to your house. My guess is you'd go all out. But the second meaning is just as important: to receive any guest the way Jesus Christ would receive them. My guess is he'd go all out.

In today's text, John says, "you are faithful in what you are doing for the brothers and sisters, even though they are strangers to you" (NIV). I imagine he could say, "You are receiving them like Christ."

I think the key here is "strangers." These weren't just random unknown people; they were other believers. As we'll see tomorrow, someone in John's friend's church was not okay with strangers coming through. It's still a problem today. If we're honest, we all have our theological turf wars, be it our denomination, our theology, our church, our culture, our politics, our zip code, or even our Sunday school class.

But go back and reread today's text and you'll find three truths about what happens when we encounter someone in the faith who's not like us:

1. They're for the Lord.
2. You're faithful if you care for them.
3. They'll tell others what you did.

If you visit the Abbey of Gethsemani, be sure to hike the trail to the sculpture garden. There you'll find a large sculpture of the three disciples who fell asleep while Jesus was praying the night he was betrayed, and about a stone's throw away you'll find a haunting statue of Jesus praying in agony.

The sculptures were donated to the Catholic monastery in memory of a white Episcopal seminarian named Jonathan Daniels who was killed in 1965 at a civil rights protest in Alabama. He was shot while shielding a black woman named Ruby Sales. On the plaque commemorating the statues is the inscription: "May we always remember that the church exists to lead men to Christ in many and varied ways, but it is always the same Christ."

### The Prayer

Heavenly Father, your Word tells us to show hospitality to strangers because they might be angels, and that when we serve the least we are serving Christ. Create in us a heart that welcomes our brothers and sisters, so that we may always receive them as Christ. In his name we pray, amen.

### The Questions

- What would it look like for you to receive someone not like you in the faith as Jesus? What would it look like for you to receive someone not in the faith like Jesus?

# 8 Don't Be That Guy

3 JOHN 9–10 | I wrote to the church about this, but Diotrephes, who loves to be the leader, refuses to have anything to do with us. When I come, I will report some of the things he is doing and the evil accusations he is making against us. Not only does he refuse to welcome the traveling teachers, he also tells others not to help them. And when they do help, he puts them out of the church.

### Consider This

Several years ago I fully experienced the horror that is church politics. I heard a lot about it and had even seen it from the outside looking in. But this time I was in the middle of it. Decisions were made in secret, lies were told, and friendships undone in the name of self-preservation. And this was between pastors.

My insides were melted. I cried for days. Then I called my dad and explained to him what was going on. My father had recently retired from a career in petroleum engineering in the Middle East where he had seen some of the worst of the worst in business politics.

"Well, son," he said, "now you know how the world works."

"But this is the church," I said, "I thought it was supposed to be different."

"Well, son," he said, "now you know the church is no different than the world."

I was cut to the quick. My father is not a Christian, and this was the church's testimony to him. But he was wrong. It was worse than the world, because these plays for power were dressed up with Bible verses and declarations of "God's will" and "We're praying for you."

Today's text shows us that church politics has been a problem since the early days. Yesterday we saw the church where John's friend worshiped had been welcoming strangers. But today we see it appears that one of the more influential members, Diotrephes, was playing church politics. On top of making evil (read: false) accusations, John says: "Not only does he refuse to welcome the traveling teachers, he also tells others not to help them. And when they do help, he puts them out of the church."

So here's my prophetic word to anyone like Diotrephes: Don't be that guy.

We know virtually nothing about Diotrephes. We don't know his backstory or his role in the church, but we know enough. We know because John tells us he "loves to be the leader." My guess is the visiting teachers were threatening his turf. And if there's one thing we've learned about politics, it's that when someone loves to be the leader, self-preservation at the expense of others becomes the name of the game.

Don't be that guy.

Because it's all the more damaging when the nature of the gospel is self-sacrifice for the sake of others.

We could correct this by saying, "Right, don't be that guy, because the church is supposed to be about love." But what does that mean? Diotrephes was about love—for himself. You can have love in your church and it still be nothing about Jesus.

So what's our metric for love? It's found in the most famous wedding Scripture that has nothing to do with a wedding: 1 Corinthians 13. In 1 Corinthians 12 Paul talks about having all the roles and results of church leadership, but without love it is just noise. Then he gives us the definition of love we're looking for:

> Love is patient and kind. Love is not jealous or boastful or proud or rude. It does not demand its own way. It is not irritable, and it keeps no record of being wronged. It does not rejoice about injustice but rejoices whenever the truth wins out. Love never gives up, never

loses faith, is always hopeful, and endures through every circumstance. (vv. 4–7)

Here's an exercise to put in your Bible, tape to your mirror, or hang on your fridge: Write down each description of love, then cross out "love is" and insert "am I?" or "do I?" It will look like this:

Am I patient?
Am I kind?
Am I jealous?
Am I boastful?
Am I proud?
Am I rude?
Do I demand my own way?
Am I irritable?
Do I keep a record of wrongs?
Do I rejoice in injustice?
Do I rejoice when truth wins?
Do I give up?
Do I lose faith?
Am I always hopeful?
Do I endure through every circumstance?

So take inventory, because the world is watching. This is not a self-serving love. It is a love for others because Christ first loved us and gave his life for us. We call it holy love.

Be that guy (or girl).

### The Prayer

Heavenly Father, we confess that we often look out for ourselves at the expense of others. By the power of the Holy Spirit, continue to transform your church—bit by bit—into having the perfect, holy love of your Son Jesus. Amen.

### The Question

• Did you do the inventory exercise? There's fifteen questions there.

# 9 When Jesus Loves You, but I Don't Have To

**3 JOHN 11–12 NIV** | Dear friend, do not imitate what is evil but what is good. Anyone who does what is good is from God. Anyone who does what is evil has not seen God. Demetrius is well spoken of by everyone—and even by the truth itself. We also speak well of him, and you know that our testimony is true.

### Consider This

"The problem with community is people," my friend said right after we'd listened to a sermon on the importance of being in a church community. And that's what John is addressing in this tiny, private letter to his friend: division in the community. Yesterday we met the one causing problems in this church, Diotrephes. John essentially tells his friend, don't be that guy: "Dear friend, do not imitate what is evil but what is good" (v. 11 NIV).

Today John introduces the one who is the opposite end of the spectrum, Demetrius. He's the example to follow because, "Demetrius is well spoken of by everyone—and even by the truth itself" (v. 12 NIV).

So what is the truth that speaks and the good we can follow? This is a private letter, so I'm going to go out on a limb and say that John's friend would be familiar with John's other writings and teachings. We have them, and I'm looking at 1 John 2:4: "If someone claims, 'I know God,' but doesn't obey God's commandments, that person is a liar and is not living in the truth."

What is the commandment? 1 John 2:7: "Dear friends, I am not writing a new commandment for you; rather it is an old one you have had from the very beginning. This old commandment—to love one another—is the same message you heard before."

But there's a caveat. First John 2:9–10: "If anyone claims, 'I am living in the light,' but hates a fellow believer, that person is still living in darkness. Anyone who loves a fellow believer is living in the light and does not cause others to stumble."

He's describing the difference between Diotrephes and Demetrius. He's describing the difference between me and someone else in my church; between you and someone else in your church. If we're honest, in some cases we're Diotrephes, and in some we're Demetrius, and sometimes we're both at the same time.

There's a reason a big chunk of the New Testament deals with the issues and sins that come between us. Because the biggest problem with community is the posture, "Jesus loves you, I don't have to." Tomorrow we'll see the biggest beauty about community, but until then I'll let the late Thomas Merton have the final word: "As long as we are on earth, the love that unites us will bring us suffering by our very contact with one another, because this love is the resetting of a Body of broken bones."[5]

### The Prayer

Jesus, I confess sometimes my posture is, "Jesus loves you, I don't have to." Forgive me, and free me to love others as you love me. This means you love me while I'm still a sinner, so I really need your help on this one. Amen.

### The Questions

- What is it you love about your community? What is it you hate about your community? Where is holy love resetting your community's broken bones?

---

5.  Thomas Merton, *New Seeds of Contemplation* (New York: New Directions, 2007), 72.

# Getting the Band Back Together

**10**

**3 JOHN 13–15** | I have much more to say to you, but I don't want to write it with pen and ink. For I hope to see you soon, and then we will talk face to face.

Peace be with you.

Your friends here send you their greetings. Please give my personal greetings to each of our friends there.

### Consider This

"Daddy, put your phone down and play with your daughters!" my daughters tell me all too often. It's a battle, especially because one of my goals as a father is to be more present with my girls. But moments like this remind me I may technically be present, but it doesn't mean I'm attentive.

I've overwhelmed with how connected I am. Every day I read dozens of blogs and hundreds of tweets; send and receive countless texts; comment, like, and share endlessly among my friends on Facebook and Instagram. But my mind and soul don't have the bandwidth to process this much stuff (and I don't think they were created to). I can put my phone down and notice that I've been connected all day, but I'm really alone.

In today's text John finishes his letter with, "I have much more to say to you, but I don't want to write it with pen and ink. For I hope to see you soon, and then we will talk face to face." If he were writing today, I imagine he could say, "I have much more to text and forward to you, but I'll wait until we can talk face-to-face."

As a pastor, as a parent, as a person, I need face-to-face. Or at least voice to voice. My soul suffers if discipleship only happens consuming online content. For me, true discipleship happens with my bandmates. I connect with two other guys on a conference call every Monday morning at 8:30 (we're old friends who now live in different states).

We start off with a simple declaration. One of us will say, "Awake o sleeper, and rise from the dead" and the other two respond, "and Christ will shine on you." Then we each take turns answering some questions about the possibility, problems, and process in the discipleship of our lives: How is it with your soul? What are your struggles and successes? How might the Holy Spirit and Scripture be speaking in your life? Do you have any sin you want to confess? Are there any secrets or hidden things you need to share?[6]

This isn't accountability partners, a small group, or a prayer circle (though those things do take place). This isn't a Bible study with a moment for prayer requests at the end. This is deeper than that. During this time we openly share fears and joys, confess sins and sorrows, declare each other forgiven

---

6. Seedbed defines "banded discipleship" as a group of 3–5 people who read together, pray together, and meet together to become the love of God for one another and the world. Learn more at discipleshipbands.com.

and beloved, and tell each other Scripture as we pray for each other. Our marriages and kids, hidden sins and habits, temptations and mental issues—over time all of life comes up. Yes, we text and e-mail each other all the time. But once a week, in a sense, we put it all down and meet face-to-face. Band together versus bandwidth.

Bands were a central part of the Methodist movement when it was still a movement. We don't really do them much anymore, if we even know what they are. But they can be a central part of the beauty of life in community: the place where deep and decisive spiritual transformation can take place together.

So, how is it with your soul? Maybe it's time to get the band back together.

### The Prayer

Heavenly Father, you created us in your image, which means the communion of the Trinity. Bring those people into our lives that we can band together with in holy communion, that we would be made holy for the sake of our souls, and for the gospel. Amen.

### The Questions

- Do you have anyone you band together with? What would this look like for you? For your soul?

# 11 Let's Give Them Something to Talk About

PHILEMON 1–6 | This letter is from Paul, a prisoner for preaching the Good News about Christ Jesus, and from our brother Timothy.

I am writing to Philemon, our beloved co-worker, and to our sister Apphia, and to our fellow soldier Archippus, and to the church that meets in your house.

May God our Father and the Lord Jesus Christ give you grace and peace.

I always thank my God when I pray for you, Philemon, because I keep hearing about your faith in the Lord Jesus and your love for all of God's people. And I am praying that you will put into action the generosity that comes from your faith as you understand and experience all the good things we have in Christ.

### Consider This

People are talking about you.

It's an ugly truth, and no matter how many sermons, Bible studies, and tweets we hear about the sin of gossip, it's still happening. It's a sin we all share in and all suffer from. So if people are going to talk about you anyway, then give them something to talk about.

Today's letter is from Paul to his friend Philemon, and I've never, ever heard a sermon preached from it. Until this Daily Text assignment, Philemon had been little more to me than a name in the litany of, "Can you name every book in the Bible?"

But this little letter packs a very important punch for letting our walk match our talk. And Paul starts this powerful letter to his friend with, "I'm hearing things about you."

What is the gossip? "I keep hearing about your faith in the Lord Jesus and your love for all of God's people" (v. 5).

I once heard the definition of a saint as, "Someone you can't talk about without talking about Jesus." It's a tall order, to be sure, and sometimes people do say false things about us. But most often when we gossip—or people gossip about us—the talk is about something negative. But what if we lived a life where people were compelled to talk more about the love of Jesus when our name came up?

In the church I pastor, my usual benediction is, "May the Holy Spirit so fill you with holy love, that when people talk about you they have to talk about how much Jesus loves us." I'm not all there yet (just ask my wife and my congregation), but I'm praying to be. If we're moving from sinner to saint, what does that look like?

### The Prayer

Heavenly Father, you spoke and created the heavens and the earth. Your Word says the power of life and death is in what I say. May the Holy Spirit so work in my life and fill me with holy love that when others talk about me or I talk about them, people have to talk about how much your Son Jesus Christ loves us. In his name, I pray. Amen.

### The Question

· What do you hope people say about you as it relates to the gospel?

# 12 Are You Childlike or Childish?

**PHILEMON 7–9** | Your love has given me much joy and comfort, my brother, for your kindness has often refreshed the hearts of God's people.

That is why I am boldly asking a favor of you. I could demand it in the name of Christ because it is the right thing for you to do. But because of our love, I prefer simply to ask you. Consider this as a request from me—Paul, an old man and now also a prisoner for the sake of Christ Jesus.

### Consider This

Paul is getting ready to ask his dear friend Philemon for something big. Something that is going to have major implications for his life, the life of a slave, and for the gospel. Paul has the authority and the power to tell Philemon what to do, but instead he writes: "I could demand it in the name of Christ because it is the right thing for you to do. But because of our love, I prefer simply to ask you" (vv. 8–9).

Think of the importance of Paul's approach this way: One of the big lessons we work on (a lot) in our house is not just what we say, but also how we say it. As I write this, my daughters are ages ten, eight, and four, so this is an ongoing lesson. The most common lesson revolves around asking for something.

For example, if one of our kids shouts, "I want a banana!" and throws a tantrum, my wife says, "I'm sorry, I can't hear you." Eventually they learn and relearn to calmly say, "Mommy, may I please have a banana?" It takes constant vigilance and work, because for kids it's natural to default to immature demanding and anger. But it can also go the other way.

One night at the dinner table, my then three-year-old didn't get what she demanded, and so turned on a big frown and started grunting in protest. My wife said, "I'm sorry, I can't hear you," while I started laughing because I thought my daughter looked and sounded like me. I turned to my wife and said, "I can't believe my three-year-old already acts like a forty-one-year-old." My wife replied, "Or maybe my forty-one-year-old acts like a three-year-old." Burn.

How we say something to someone is just as important as what we're saying. We are ready to teach and reteach this lesson to our children, but sometimes we need to learn and relearn it ourselves.

Our current conversational climate is hostile and toxic, especially when talking about the two things we're not supposed to talk about in polite company: politics and religion.

We've probably all seen that our tweets, posts, and comments demanding people see our side or believe our cause and then throwing a kind of tantrum when they don't is, well, childish. And what do almost all of us do when approached with childish demands? "I'm sorry, I can't hear you." None of this is helpful with the urgency and importance of the gospel we're called to share in love.

*I could demand it in the name of Christ because it is the right thing for you to do. But because of our love, I prefer simply to ask you.*

Tomorrow we'll see that Paul, in a sense, is going to dive into a hot political and theological issue with his friend. But, first, he's going to be sure it's not just what he says, but how he says it. After all, in Paul's other letter to the same town where Philemon lives, he writes: "Pray . . . that God will give us many opportunities to speak about his mysterious plan concerning Christ. . . . Let your conversation be gracious and attractive so you will have the right response for everyone" (Col. 4:3, 6).

Because maybe part of having faith like a child, rather than being childish, is to be retaught some of our childhood lessons.

### The Prayer

Jesus, you said to have faith like a child. Help me to remember that the power of life and death is in what I say and in how I say it. May the words of my mouth be full of life, bearing fruit, and pleasing to you. In your name I pray, amen.

### The Questions

- How do you think the good news of Jesus has been lost to the way we talk to each other? What would it look like for your conversations to be "gracious and attractive"?

# A Little Less Conversation, a Little More Action

# 13

PHILEMON 10–14 NIV | I appeal to you for my son Onesimus, who became my son while I was in chains. Formerly he was useless to you, but now he has become useful both to you and to me.

I am sending him—who is my very heart—back to you. I would have liked to keep him with me so that he could take your place in helping me while I am in chains for the gospel. But I did not want to do anything without your consent, so that any favor you do would not seem forced but would be voluntary.

## Consider This

The flattery and talking is done, and now it's time to get down to kingdom business. At the start of this letter Paul told his friend Philemon: "I am praying you will put into action the generosity that comes from your faith . . ." (v. 6).

In other words, it's time for a little less conversation and little more action. And the action here is about dealing with a slave of Philemon's named Onesimus.

We need to take a sidebar here and talk about slavery and Scripture. First, we must acknowledge that certain scriptures (including these from Philemon) have been misused and abused to perpetuate the sin of slavery in our history. This is wrong.

Second, context is everything. We must remember that slavery in the Roman Empire was not the same as slavery in the Confederate South. Slaves were often given the chance to be educated, many were paid wages and could buy their own freedom, many were given freedom at a certain age. In fact, some slaves owned slaves of their own, and many bought and sold themselves into and out of slavery depending on their economic situation.[7] But make no mistake, it was still slavery, which meant the lowest level of status for a human in the empire.

It is into this reality that Paul the prisoner releases Onesimus the slave. We don't know why he ran away, but it

---

7. Paul J. Achtemeier, Joel B. Green, and Marianne Meye Thompson, *Introducing the New Testament: Its Literature and Theology* (Grand Rapids, MI: William B. Eerdmans Publishing, 2001), 425.

seems at some point Onesimus connected with Paul, became a believer, and had been helping him ever since. Now Paul is sending him back. Under Roman law, this would have been really bad news for Onesimus. There were laws in place that allowed for severe punishment for returned slaves. So then why would Paul do this?

To paraphrase the late Robert Mulholland, your ministry is not so much what you say, it is who you are with others, and who you are with others depends on who you are with Jesus. In other words, it's time for a little less conversation, and a little more action.

Paul is about to ask Philemon to receive Onesimus differently than the culture or the law would: as someone sacred based on who they are in Christ. And, remember, Paul addressed this letter not only to Philemon, but to the entire congregation. He's asking all of them to do something unheard of, something radical, where the first are last and the last are first; where the way down is the way up.

Philemon is a believer, and how he receives Onesimus will reveal who he is with Jesus. In a great twist of poetic irony, these scriptures that in the past have been used to justify slavery are actually Paul working to set slaves free. I believe that's why Paul is doing this. And in the key setup, Paul says: "But I did not want to do anything without your consent, so that any favor you do would not seem forced but would be voluntary" (v. 14).

I once heard Billy Abraham say, "If you can't say no, then your yes is meaningless."[8] It is only in the freedom and holy love of Jesus that Philemon—or any of us—can be willing to do something unheard of for the gospel. It's time for a little less conversation and a little more action (please).

### The Prayer

Heavenly Father, by the power of your Holy Spirit, would you guide us along the path of truth, for your name's sake? Through Jesus Christ our Lord. Amen.

### The Question

- What does it mean for you to be willing, instead of forced, to do the will of the Father?

# 14 Why Would I Do That?

PHILEMON 15–17 | It seems you lost Onesimus for a little while so that you could have him back forever. He is no longer like a slave to you. He is more than a slave, for he is a beloved brother, especially to me. Now he will mean much more to you, both as a man and as a brother in the Lord.

So if you consider me your partner, welcome him as you would welcome me.

---

8. Billy Abraham, keynote address at Refresh Conference, December 15, 2009. Woodlands United Methodist Church, The Woodlands, Texas.

### Consider This

Paul has asked a tall favor of his dear friend: for Philemon to show kindness to his returning slave, Onesimus. Remember, yesterday we learned there were laws allowing severe punishment for runaway slaves. But Paul doesn't stop at kindness, he goes all the way for liberation: "He is no longer like a slave to you. He is more than a slave, for he is a beloved brother . . . Now he will mean much more to you, both as a man and as a brother in the Lord" (v. 16).

I can hear Philemon saying, "Yeah, but why?" And I believe Paul's answer would be would begin with the word "submission."

Submission is one of those "DANGER: Do Not Touch" words in polite theological circles, especially because of the way certain Scripture passages have been used in relation to wives and women. Submission is the laying down of a person's will, desires, rights, and entitlements to the will of another for the other person's sake. Submission is at the heart of what Paul is asking Philemon to do—and what the gospel is asking us to do.

Yeah, but why?

Paul makes his case in Ephesians:

> Submit to one another out of reverence for Christ. For wives, this means submit to your husbands as to the Lord. . . . For husbands, this means love your wives, just as Christ loved the church. He gave up his life for her . . . (5:21–22, 25)

> Children, obey your parents because you belong to the Lord, for this is the right thing to do. . . . [Parents], do not provoke your children to anger by the way you treat them. Rather, bring them up with the discipline and instruction that comes from the Lord. . . .
>
> Slaves, obey your earthly masters with deep respect and fear. Serve them sincerely as you would serve Christ. . . . Masters, treat your slaves in the same way. Don't threaten them; remember, you both have the same Master in heaven, and he has no favorites. (6:1, 4–5, 9)

See what Paul is doing here? He's laying down the case that all our relationships are about submission to each other. In fact, he begins with this all important statement: submit to one another. And most important to notice: each submission is tied to what one believes about the Lord.

Yeah, but why? Because as Paul says in Philippians 2:5–8:

> You must have the same attitude that Christ Jesus had.
>> Though he was God,
>>> he did not think of equality with God
>>> as something to cling to.
>> Instead, he gave up his divine privileges;
>>> he took the humble position of a slave
>>> and was born as a human being.
>> When he appeared in human form,
>>> he humbled himself in obedience to God
>>> and died a criminal's death on a cross.

Do you see it? Jesus gave up his will, desires, rights, and entitlements, and submitted to taking the humble position of a slave . . . and died a criminal's death on a cross.

In other words, how does a slave owner submit to his slave?

(Short sidebar in the argument of wives submitting to husbands and husbands loving their wives as Christ loved the church: this Philippians passage shows us what Christ's love looks like. So who is called to the greater act of submission?)

Paul echoes the same case in his letter to the Colossians, which happens to be the same city and church where Philemon lived and worshiped, so he probably heard this teaching. Why does this matter? This was about a slave two thousand years ago. Should you care? If so, why?

Because whether we're talking about the equality of women, the welcoming of immigrants, the rescuing of refugees, the health of the poor—there are no favorites; no second-class citizens. When it comes to sharing the good news the message to Philemon is the same as to us:

> You are all children of God through faith in Christ Jesus. And all who have been united with Christ in baptism have put on Christ, like putting on new clothes. There is no longer Jew or Gentile, slave or free, male and female. For you are all one in Christ Jesus. (Gal. 3:26–28)

### The Prayer

Heavenly Father, this is more than a tough idea to grasp or lesson to learn. This is a hard thing to live, but this is good news. Help us to have the mind of Christ in laying down our will, desires, rights, and entitlements for the sake of holy love. In Jesus' name we pray, amen.

### The Questions

- Where do you need to submit to another person out of faith in Jesus Christ? Why?

# 15 Show Me, Don't Tell Me

PHILEMON 18–25 NIV | If he has done you any wrong or owes you anything, charge it to me. I, Paul, am writing this with my own hand. I will pay it back—not to mention that you owe me your very self. I do wish, brother, that I may have some benefit from you in the Lord; refresh my heart in Christ. Confident of your obedience, I write to you, knowing that you will do even more than I ask.

And one thing more: Prepare a guest room for me, because I hope to be restored to you in answer to your prayers.

Epaphras, my fellow prisoner in Christ Jesus, sends you greetings. And so do Mark, Aristarchus, Demas and Luke, my fellow workers.

The grace of the Lord Jesus Christ be with your spirit.

### Consider This

Just the other day, my wife came home from running errands and asked if I had read the latest Daily Text. Of course I had, I told her, because I've been the substitute Daily Texter! I didn't just read it, I wrote it. She knew that, but said, "Just checking, because you really need to do what it says. I love you!"

I smiled and told my wife I love her too. She wants to hear it, but she really wants to see it: in how I am present with our daughters when I get home from work, or in how I budget our money, or when I clean the toilets or put down my iPhone. You get the idea.

In other words: show me, don't tell me.

Paul began this letter by telling his friend "I am praying that you will put into action the generosity that comes from your faith . . ." (v. 6). Yesterday we looked at Paul talking about submission in Colossians and Ephesians, and how Philemon would have been familiar with this teaching. But in this letter he's challenging Philemon to not just know about submission, but to put it into practice.

In other words: show me, don't tell me.

In today's text, at the end of the letter, we get Paul doing the same. A runaway slave would have cost Philemon a lot, but Paul finishes all Christlike when he says: "If he has done you any wrong or owes you anything, charge it to me. . . . I will pay it back" (vv. 18–19 NIV).

This entire letter is Paul using his authority in love to challenge Philemon to rethink what it means to be a servant of Christ. And he does this by redefining Philemon's relationship to his slave Onesimus. The goal of the gospel is to redefine our relationship to God, to others, and even to ourselves. If, as we've already seen, the first half of the gospel is John 3:16—"For this is how God loved the world: He gave his one and only Son, so that everyone who believes in him will not perish but have eternal life"—and the second half of the gospel is 1 John 3:16—"We know what real love is because Jesus gave up his life for us. So we also ought to give up our lives for our brothers and sisters"—then the whole gospel can be summed up in: show me, don't tell me.

In his introduction to Philemon, Eugene Peterson says, "Every movement we make in response to God has a ripple effect, touching family, neighbors, friends, community. Belief in God alters our language. Love of God affects daily relationships . . . it all gets worked into local history, eventually into world history."[9]

So my charge to you as we finish this letter is the same as Paul's to Philemon: "Confident of your obedience, I write to you, knowing that you will do even more than I ask" (v. 21 NIV).

In other words: show me, don't tell me.

### The Prayer

Heavenly Father, stir up the gift of your Holy Spirit in our lives so that when we tell people Jesus loves them, we show it too. In your Son's name we pray, amen.

---

9. Eugene Peterson, *The Message: The Bible in Contemporary Language* (Colorado Springs, CO: NavPress, 2004), 1394.

### The Questions

- What would it look like for your relationship with Christ to redefine some of your personal relationships? Can you not just tell people Jesus loves them, but show it?

# This Is Personal

# 16

**TITUS 1:1** | This letter is from Paul, a slave of God and an apostle of Jesus Christ. I have been sent to proclaim faith of those God has chosen and to teach them to know the truth that shows them how to live godly lives.

### Consider This

"Because Jesus is good news and Jesus is in me, I am good news."

This is a line from our Seedbed Sower's Creed. I've never thought about it before, but I think it sums up the aim of most of the New Testament. Think about it: The word *gospel* means "good news," and the four Gospels (Matthew, Mark, Luke, and John) tell us the good news of Jesus Christ and how his birth, life, death, resurrection, ascension, and promised return free us from sin and death.

That's the good news for *everyone, everywhere.*

And the book of Acts (also knows as the Gospel of Luke, Part Two) tells us how that good news spread from Jerusalem to the Roman Empire, which eventually spread around the globe (which includes you reading this right now).

But, for the most part, the bulk of the rest of the New Testament is made up of letters that are specifically addressed *only* to believers. The letters of Paul, John, Peter, James, Jude—all inside information. Written for Christians' eyes only for one reason and one reason only: to strengthen the "faith to those God has chosen and to teach them to know the truth that shows them how to live godly lives."

In other words, they were written because Jesus is good news, and Jesus was in their readers, and they had to learn how to become good news.

As we've seen in 2 John (and will see in Jude), these letters address a lot of false teachings from without and within. They deal with all the stuff that gets in the way of us being good news and encourage us in the things that make us good news. Today we start a very personal letter Paul wrote to one person: Titus.

A personal letter carries more weight; it has a different tone. Because of this, we're not going to like everything we hear. That's why the first four verses we look at over these first three days are of utmost importance. They are the foundation of everything else we hope to hear from the Lord in Titus.

And what we need to hear is good news.

### The Prayer

Jesus, you are good news and you are in me. Help me become good news for others. Amen.

### The Question

- Are you ready to get personal in order to be the good news of Jesus?

# Anytime. Anywhere.

**17**

TITUS 1:2–3 | **This truth gives them confidence that they have eternal life, which God—who does not lie—promised them before the world began. And now at just the right time he has revealed this message, which we announce to everyone. It is by the command of God our Savior that I have been entrusted with this work for him.**

### Consider This

It's everywhere. On notebooks and throw pillows and coffee mugs. It's one of the standards for major life events from dedication to confirmation to graduation. It's the go-to verse for many looking for the silver lining in difficult times: "'For I know the plans I have for you,' says the LORD. 'They are plans for good and not for disaster, to give you a future and a hope'" (Jer. 29:11).

But back up a few verses, and we see a bleaker picture: God's people are foreigners in a land they never wanted to live in and can't wait to get out of, among a people who burned their homes and temple to the ground, slaughtered their loved ones, and took them as prisoners into exile. This was never part of the plan, but it's in this setting that the Lord says:

> "Build homes, and plan to stay. Plant gardens, and eat the food they produce. Marry and have children. Then find spouses for them so that you may have many grandchildren. Multiply! Do not dwindle away! And work for the peace and prosperity of the city where I sent you into exile. Pray to the Lord for it, for its welfare will determine your welfare." (Jer. 29:5–7)

Only after he tells them to work for the well-being of their enemies does God go on to say he has plans to give them a future and a hope. Not exactly graduation card material, eh?

Acts 27 tells the story of Paul under arrest for his faith, a prisoner on a boat bound for Rome that is shipwrecked in bad weather on Crete. We don't know how long he's there or what he did. But the Lord must have done something through them during that time because Paul says he wrote this letter to Titus, whom he left "on the island of Crete so you could complete our work there and appoint elders [church leaders] in each town . . ." (Titus 1:5).

In today's text, Paul says God has revealed his message of how to live a godly life at "just the right time." Now being taken prisoner and shipwrecked may never have been part of the plan, but there's Paul and Titus at just the right time and place for the revelation of what God was doing.

So when is the right time and where is the right place for us to live godly lives and share the gospel? Answer: anytime and anywhere.

In Colossians 4:3–5 Paul writes:

> Pray for us, too, that God will give us many opportunities to speak about his mysterious plan concerning Christ. That is why I am here in chains. Pray that I will proclaim this message as clearly as I should. Live wisely among those who are not believers, and make the most of every opportunity.

Anytime. Anywhere. Especially in the times and places that don't go as planned, because that seems to be where the Lord shows up. The situation of our hearts and circumstances of our lives don't have to be perfect or sailing smoothly. They usually aren't, anyway (you know, the whole "when I am weak you are strong" reality).

Yesterday I introduced a line from the Seedbed Sower's Creed. Today let's make the whole creed our prayer for anytime and anywhere.

### *The Prayer*

Today, I sow for a great awakening.

Today, I stake everything on the promise of the Word of God. I depend entirely on the power of the Holy Spirit. I have the same mind in me that was in Christ Jesus. Because Jesus is good news and Jesus is in me, I am good news.

Today, I will sow the extravagance of the gospel everywhere I go and into everyone I meet.

Today, I will love others as Jesus has loved me.

Today, I will remember that the tiniest seeds become the tallest trees; that the seeds of today become the shade of tomorrow; that the faith of right now becomes the future of the everlasting kingdom.

Today, I sow for a great awakening.

### The Questions

- Ever hear the old adage of when's the best time to plant an oak tree? Twenty years ago. When's the second-best time? Right now. So where can you sow today?

# 18 | We Can Do Hard Things

TITUS 1:4 | I am writing to Titus, my true son in the faith that we share.

May God the Father and Christ Jesus our Savior give you grace and peace.

### Consider This

During a particularly rough patch in college I got a letter from my grandmother, Granny Boyd. I won't get into the details, but her handwritten note has some great lines that still speak to me today:

"You have persevered where many with ADD have dropped out. You deserve a lot of credit."

"No one likes to have one disaster after another . . . but you learned something."

"It was gut-wrenching, and it is hard to suddenly realize it is over, but it is time to move on. Those days are just a memory."

"P. S. I'll also pray you get a car."

Her counsel starts off encouraging, but in the second half she brings it down. She knew I was in a hard place, but she also knew I could (and needed to) do hard things. If someone else had said those same words to me in the same difficult situation, I know I would have become angry and defensive. And if I had heard that same kind of general advice in a sermon, I would have ignored it.

But these words were from my Granny, who had almost single-handedly prayed me through college. I loved her deeply and she loved me, and because of that love she could tell me hard things.

In today's text, Paul calls Titus his "true son in the faith that we share." Paul had left Titus in Crete with a very hard mission: find local people to lead new churches in a pagan culture. But Titus was someone Paul had invested his life in; someone Paul loved very much, so he could say hard things to his "son." That is why this letter is going to have a different tenor and feel than say, a sermon Paul would send to the church in Rome.

Given his calling, Titus would need to be challenged. Paul was calling Titus to a life that would call others to a life that the culture did not want. It was too black and white. Paul is going to say some very direct and culturally controversial stuff in the rest of this letter, but if we keep his heart and his aim in front of us then the content of the rest of the letter holds.

We should expect God to speak both words of building up *and* words of challenge because of the depth of his love for us. Consider Hebrews 12:5–6: "My dear child, don't shrug off God's discipline, but don't be crushed by it either. It's the child he loves that he disciplines; the child he embraces, he also corrects" (MSG).

If we're honest, the kind of approach we'll see in this letter is foreign to most of us, or at least uncomfortable. But hard words are not the problem. Having a heart that won't receive them is. My posture toward my Granny's letter was, *I know who is writing this, and her heart toward me is love, so I can receive it.*

God says hard words because he is calling us to a life that calls others to a life that the culture does not want. Keep coming back to today's post to remind us and help us take the posture that says, *I know who is writing this, and their heart for me is Jesus. And their heart is for the kingdom of God to come on earth as it is in heaven. So I can receive hard words and do hard things.*

### The Prayer

Jesus, because your heart for me is love, help me to receive hard words and do hard things, by the power of your Holy Spirit. Amen.

### The Question

- Is there someone in your life who, between the two of you, can say and hear hard things in love?

# Respect Your Eldership 19

TITUS 1:5–7 NIV | The reason I left you in Crete was that you might put in order what was left unfinished and appoint elders in every town, as I directed you. An elder must be blameless, faithful to his wife, a man whose children believe and are not open to the charge of being wild and disobedient. Since an overseer manages God's household, he must be blameless—not overbearing, not quick-tempered, not given to drunkenness, not violent, not pursuing dishonest gain.

### Consider This

On June 4, 2018, I knelt at the altar as my wife, my two oldest daughters, other pastors, and our bishop laid their hands on my head and shoulders. Then the bishop said, "Almighty God, pour upon Omar Hamid Al-Rikabi the Holy Spirit, for the office and work of an elder in Christ's holy church."

Then I placed my hand on a Bible and my younger daughter started to rub my back as the bishop continued: "Omar take authority as an elder to preach the Word of God, to administer the Holy Sacraments, and to order the life of the church in the name of the Father, and of the Son, and of the Holy Spirit."

And just like that, I was ordained. But not really just like that. This moment was the culmination of years of seminary education, written examinations, psychological evaluations, church evaluations, residency, oral examinations, and lots and lots of other qualifications that led many of us to call this journey "ordination purgatory."

But for better or worse, the system is set up to make sure ordination is not just given on a whim for the men and women called to lead the church.

After Paul and Titus were shipwrecked on Crete, some kind of ministry happened because Paul sailed on and left Titus to find local leaders for new churches in a pagan land. And he starts off by listing a set of basic qualifications to lead.

Now, this is where we can veer off into a debate about what this list means for pastors and church leaders today. Some seem kind of obvious, but how many pastors today have been divorced? Or how many reading this now have a wry smile because they were once the stereotypical preacher's kid? Why doesn't Paul say anything about elders not sacrificing their families on the altar of ministry? And really, who among us is fully blameless?

There is much that could be said and debated about the culture and climate Titus was in versus what the church is like today. So is this list specifically for elders in first-century Crete, for official clergy today, or for all of us?

To answer this we need to go back to the Old Testament, so stick with me here. In the Old Testament, the priests ran the temple, and their primary job was to create space for God's people to worship, offer sacrifices, and teach the Law.

In other words, the priests were the mediators between God and humanity. This is summed up in Hebrews 5:1, 4: "Every high priest is a man chosen to represent other people in their dealings with God. He presents their gifts to God and offers sacrifices for their sins. . . . And no one can become a high priest simply because he wants such an honor. He must be called by God for this work."

There were also purity rules for priests that echo Paul's list for elders (see Leviticus 21). And by the time we get to today's text, Paul is talking about the evolution from priest to elder. Different titles, but the same basic call: to lead the people in worship and preaching. In another letter, Paul says, "Elders who do their work well should be respected and paid well, especially those who work hard at both preaching and teaching" (1 Tim. 5:17).

If an elder was a leader of the church called to preach and teach, this takes us back to our original question: Is this list specifically for elders in first-century Crete also for official clergy today or for all of us?

Yes. The answer is yes.

The big takeaway from the list in today's text is this: If you're called to lead, then how you live, both privately and publicly, matter. In leadership, character has always mattered.

And we're all called to lead.

Now please hear me: We haven't all been called to be the leader, but we've all been called to lead. Part of the downside of the church today is the clergy/non-clergy distinction. Through Jesus Christ all believers are temples of the Holy Spirit (see 1 Corinthians 6:19) and we are all called to offer ourselves as a living sacrifice to God as an act of worship (see Romans 12:1). Sound familiar?

Yep. We're all priests. We're all called to the work of elders to preach and teach with our lives. We're all called to be mediators between God and others: "You are royal priests, a holy nation, God's very own possession. As a result, you can show others the goodness of God, for he called you out of the darkness into his wonderful light" (1 Peter 2:9).

That's why today's text is for all of us, because character matters.

Now before we run off and hold Paul's list over others who fall short, or shrink back from our calling because of our shortcomings, remember what Hebrews 5:2–3 says in the midst of describing the priesthood: "And he [the priest] is able to deal gently with ignorant and wayward people because he himself is subject to the same weaknesses. This is why he must offer sacrifices for his own sins as well as theirs."

Because character matters. But grace matters more.

### The Prayer

Jesus, you abide in me and I abide in you. I confess to you that my character is a work in progress toward holiness. Let your grace fill in the gaps where my character needs help so that my life can show others the goodness of God. Amen.

### The Question

- Where do you see your priestly role and what is God working out in your character for that role?

# Be Our Guest

20

**TITUS 1:8** | Rather, he must enjoy having guests in his home, and he must love what is good. He must live wisely and be just. He must live a devout and disciplined life.

### Consider This

It sounds so pleasant, but "he must enjoy having guests in his home" is not a call for more dinner parties. In fact, the rules of Middle Eastern hospitality that run through the Bible make this a hard statement.

Consider the parable Jesus tells in Luke 11. He's teaching about prayer, but the story is also a window into biblical hospitality. The scene opens with a man who has some unexpected guests show up in the middle of the night. He has no bread (the staple food item) to feed them, so he goes over to a friend's house to ask for some.

Now, this is not the same as running next door to borrow a cup of sugar. First, it's the middle of the night and in those days the friend would be sleeping on the floor right next to the rest of his family. Second, only enough bread for the day was baked fresh early in the morning. So to give some bread would have been either a hassle to make or robbed him of whatever leftovers he had.

But here's the deal: There were strict codes of hospitality in the biblical Middle East that obligated a host to provide any guest with food as a welcome. Not because of good manners, but because the table for meals was considered a type of altar, and to break bread with a visitor meant *you are important to me and you are now a sacred part of our family*. Furthermore, it was a great social shame to not have or give bread to a guest. The friend says to go away because it's the middle of the night and his family is asleep; he's not going to help him. But then Jesus says, "But I tell you this—though he won't do it for friendship's sake, if you keep knocking long enough, he will get up and give you whatever you need because of your shameless persistence" (Luke 11:8).

Pete Grieg, author and founder of 24–7 Prayer makes the point better than I:

> People tell me they have the gift of hospitality by which I think they mean that they like dinner parties. They have (or aspire to have) a beautiful home with an underused spare room, in which they enjoy entertaining exotic, interesting, appreciative guests who confirm just how lovely their home is.
>
> This is not the gift of hospitality. This is the gift of a box of chocolates. Biblical hospitality . . . is a really bad lifestyle choice. True hospitality allows for interruption, goes the second mile and above all it is present to people. . . . It can often hurt our schedules,

our emotions, our bank accounts and, yes, it can even mess up our homes.[10]

Yesterday we saw Paul giving instructions for Titus to find elders (pastors) for churches; it is this kind of hard hospitality he lists as their first job description. But it's not surprising, because two chapters later in Luke's gospel Jesus is eating at someone's house and Luke writes:

> Then he turned to his host. "When you put on a luncheon or a banquet," he said, "don't invite your friends, brothers, relatives, and rich neighbors. For they will invite you back, and that will be your only reward. Instead, invite the poor, the crippled, the lame, and the blind. Then at the resurrection of the righteous, God will reward you for inviting those who could not repay you." (Luke 14:12–14)

Matthew 9:10–11 tells the story of Jesus at another meal: "Later, Matthew invited Jesus and his disciples to his home as dinner guests, along with many tax collectors and other disreputable sinners. But when the Pharisees saw this, they asked his disciples, 'Why does your teacher eat with such scum?'"

Pop application quiz: Remember two minutes ago when you read that to eat with someone meant you are important to me and you are now a sacred part of our family? That's why Jesus eats with scum, and where we find our hospitality calling.

---

10. Pete Greig Facebook Page, March 6, 2018, www.facebook.com/pete.greig1.

I love Eugene Peterson's translation in *The Message* of Jesus' response: "I'm here to invite outsiders, not coddle insiders" (v. 13).

Can you imagine if *that* was the first line of a pastor's job description, or the church's mission statement, or at least the hospitality committee's charge? It should be, because everything I just described in today's text is what happens at the table of Holy Communion. Jesus welcomes us, sinners and scum, then calls us to go and do the same. The eucharistic life is holy and hard hospitality, but as we learned two days ago, we can do hard things.

### The Prayer

Jesus, you welcome me, a sinner, to your Holy Communion table of grace. Help me give that same hospitality to everyone I meet. Amen.

### The Question

- Where is your table altar of hospitality these days?

# 21 Why So Serious?

TITUS 1:9–13A | He must have a strong belief in the trustworthy message he was taught; then he will be able to encourage others with wholesome teaching and show those who oppose it where they are wrong.

For there are many rebellious people who engage in useless talk and deceive others. This is especially true of those who insist on circumcision for salvation. They must be silenced, because they are turning whole families away from the truth by their false teaching. And they do it only for money. Even one of their own men, a prophet from Crete, has said about them, "The people of Crete are all liars, cruel animals, and lazy gluttons." This is true.

### Consider This

Recently I received a very important award. It was a "Certificate of Awesomeness" for "Chief Happiness Director and Excellence in Humor." I earned this distinction for my volunteer work at my daughters' elementary school. I think the certificate is suitable for framing, but my wife says it's just proof that my dad humor finally works (with small children, at least).

Maybe this award is really a grace outlet for me. Because I'll be honest and say that preaching and teaching and leading Bible studies and pastoral work is always such a serious endeavor that I can forget to have fun with it. Yes, we're talking about serious stuff, but didn't God create laughter?

That's the case in today's text. Yes, Paul is addressing serious stuff (it is Scripture, after all). But when Paul says, "Even one of their own men, a prophet from Crete, has said about them, 'The people of Crete are all liars, cruel animals, and lazy gluttons.' This is true," this what scholars call the "Cretan liar paradox." Paul is quoting a famous Cretan philosopher who called all Cretans liars, which meant he himself was a liar. In other words, it was a joke.

According to N. T. Wright, this was a tongue-in-cheek statement, intended to be funny: "Paul is laughing, not unkindly, but finding ways of warning Titus that he's going to have to be robust and be prepared to work with the people of Crete."[11]

As we've seen before, Paul has given Titus a serious task: to live a life that calls others to live a lifestyle that the culture doesn't want. And in today's text we see a big obstacle to that work: folks coming over to tell new Gentile believers that they have to follow specific Jewish laws and customs if they want to really be saved. Specifically, they're telling grown men they're not really saved unless they get circumcised. (Imagine being a twenty-something Greek man hearing he's got to go through that procedure to be saved. No wonder they were turning away.)

These folks were peddling fear and guarantees for attention and profit, not really discipleship or sanctification. Thankfully that's not a problem in the church today.

See what I did there? Tongue-in-cheek—just like Paul!

The point is that, yes, this is serious and eternal stuff we're talking about here. But sometimes—okay, a lot of the time—we can get so worked up debating and arguing every last theological detail *for all the wrong reasons*. But let's not. In today's culture it can be exhausting "turning whole families away."

---

11. N. T. Wright, *Paul for Everyone: The Pastoral Letters of 1 and 2 Timothy, and Titus* (Westminster: John Knox Press, Kindle Edition), 147.

Buried in the midst of this letter is grace for all of our holy seriousness. Paul is trying to be funny. He's telling a joke. It's pastor humor. But that's okay, because, after all, God began his rescue mission with a kid name Laughter.

This is serious stuff, but let's not take ourselves so seriously.

### The Prayer
Jesus, the joy of the Lord is supposed to be my strength. Help me to laugh when I am weak so I can be strong in you. Amen.

### The Question
- Heard any good jokes lately?

# But Seriously

# 22

**TITUS 1:13B–15 NIV** | Therefore rebuke them sharply, so that they will be sound in the faith and will pay no attention to Jewish myths or to the merely human commands of those who reject the truth. To the pure, all things are pure, but to those who are corrupted and do not believe, nothing is pure. In fact, both their minds and consciences are corrupted.

### Consider This
Right before I started high school, I came to faith at a Petra concert (the Christian rock band of the '80s), and not long after became a staunch believer that real Christians only listened to Christian music. Some of my friends and I gathered

together all of our non-Christian records and tapes, smashed them, and then burned them in my parents' fireplace.

A year later during a special youth service at our church, a guy we didn't really know from school chose to follow Christ. He didn't come from any church or religious background, and it was evident that his decision to follow Jesus was genuine.

The next day he joined us at the morning prayer meeting we held before school. He showed up wearing the T-shirt of a popular non-Christian heavy metal band (remember, it was the '80s). After our opening prayer, the first thing I told him was that to be a real Christian he would have to quit listening to non-Christian music. He would have to get rid of that T-shirt, and any others like it, along with all of his secular albums.

We never saw him again after that.

It might be a crude anecdote, but it is the closest real-life analogy I can think of for today's text. In yesterday's text, we saw Paul make a joke, but now he gets serious.

For some context we need to look at Galatians 2 when Paul brought Titus to Jerusalem. Titus was a Gentile convert, and apparently after they got there some of the leaders began discussing if Titus should be circumcised. But Paul wasn't having it (and I'm sure Titus was very thankful). In verse 4, Paul says these false teachers were trying to take away the freedom we have in Jesus, and that is what he is reminding Titus about today.

You see, what's really happening is these false-folks were coming to new believers and essentially saying, "You are a new convert who believes Jesus' death and resurrection forgives your sins and saves your soul, but in order for you to be a real Christian you must follow this rule on circumcision."

This is kind of a big deal because the whole idea of "saved by grace through faith" is that our salvation is not based on what we do, but who God is. It is his actions through Jesus, not ours, that initiate and fulfill the requirements for salvation. Paul rejects anyone who teaches otherwise because to do so could lead new and early-in-the-faith believers away.

And that's no joke.

### The Prayer

Jesus, help me to remember you are the one doing the saving, and save me from turning away from this truth. Amen.

### The Question

• Where do you see this kind of false-teaching at work today?

# It's Really Black-and-White

# 23

TITUS 1:16–2:3 | Such people claim they know God, but they deny him by the way they live. They are detestable and disobedient, worthless for doing anything good.

As for you, Titus, promote the kind of living that reflects wholesome teaching. Teach the older men to exercise self-control, to be worthy of respect, and to live wisely. They must have sound faith and be filled with love and patience.

Similarly, teach the older women to live in a way that honors God. They must not slander others or be heavy drinkers. Instead, they should teach others what is good.

### Consider This

In college I studied literature and history, which meant I was trained to look for things that weren't obvious from surface reading. What's the context, the world of the author, the language, the symbolism? What is the deeper meaning?

But sometimes the words just mean exactly what they say. An English professor once told our class the story of meeting Ernest Hemingway's wife at a conference. He went on and on with her about how her husband used this and that image to symbolize that and this idea, but she cut him off and said, "Ernie just wrote stories. All of you came up with all that other stuff."

In the story of Scripture, context is everything. Knowing who Paul was writing to and where, what the culture was like, and how the language was used help us better interpret and apply the Bible. But sometimes (okay, a lot of the time) we get caught up looking for the deeper meaning. (And, full disclosure, we preacher and teacher types love to try to find or see something new to preach. It's a problem.)

But sometimes there is no hidden symbolism. No deeper meaning. No having to stretch the imagination to figure out what it means for us today. Sometimes the black-and-white print is really black-and-white teaching.

Exercise self-control. Have love. Be patient. Don't slander. Don't get drunk. Teach what is good. Pretty straightforward teaching from the first to the twenty-first century.

So why do these things? For Titus, N. T. Wright sets the scene:

> But what if there's a town in the ancient Mediterranean world which has never seen Christians before? This is a new community, organizing itself in a new way, refusing to join in with normal public events like the sacrifices which celebrate the various gods and goddesses, including the special local ones. Its members no longer frequent the drunken orgies they once did. They are even rumored to refuse to take the oath of allegiance to the emperor. . . . People will be watching.[12]

Doing these things aren't about us earning our salvation or being better people. It's so that our lives reflect Jesus. So what is your scene today? Because it's still really black-and-white: people are watching.

---

12. N. T. Wright, *Paul for Everyone: The Pastoral Letters of 1 and 2 Timothy, and Titus* (Westminster: John Knox Press, Kindle Edition), 151.

### The Prayer

Jesus, it's really black-and-white: help me live a life that reflects you so that when people watch me they see how much you love the world. Amen.

### The Question

• What is your scene today, and who's watching?

# 24 A Different Time (Part One)

**TITUS 2:4–8 NIV** | Then they can urge the younger women to love their husbands and children, to be self-controlled and pure, to be busy at home, to be kind, and to be subject to their husbands, so that no one will malign the word of God.

Similarly, encourage the young men to be self-controlled. In everything set them an example by doing what is good. In your teaching show integrity, seriousness and soundness of speech that cannot be condemned, so that those who oppose you may be ashamed because they have nothing bad to say about us.

### Consider This

When my daughter Norah was in kindergarten I began a very important part of her larger education: watching *Star Wars*. This was her first non-cartoon movie and she sat perfectly still while she watched the original 1977 classic, the same one I first saw at her age.

In the end, when our heroes got their medals for blowing up the Death Star and the credits rolled, I waited for her review. After all she had just seen, she turned to me and asked, "Daddy, why is there only one girl in this movie?"

I immediately thought back to a line earlier in the movie, after that one girl, Princess Leia, had just saved her rescuers. Han Solo looks at her and offers, "If we just avoid any more female advice we ought to be able to get out of here." I cringed and tried to explain to my daughter, "Well, it was a different time."

On the surface, Paul's instruction to Titus that women should stay home and submit to their husbands makes us want to cringe and say, "Well, it was a different time."

There is some truth to that because he was writing in a hyper-patriarchal time. But that's no excuse because the patriarchy was never God's intention. Look back to the creation story in Genesis and notice where the line, "And you will desire to control your husband, but he will rule over you" (v. 16b), is situated. It's in chapter 3, right in the middle of the list of curses.

So what gives? If Paul believes what he says in all his letters about the work of Christ on the cross overcoming the curse, then what's going on here? Is Paul arguing for remaining in the curse? Not at all.

Remember, this is a personal letter between two people, Paul and Titus. We know that Titus traveled with Paul and delivered some of his other letters, so it's safe to say he was familiar with Paul's larger teachings. All this little letter is doing is jogging his memory. So what is the larger teaching?

It begins in Ephesians 5: "Submit to one another out of reverence for Christ. For wives, this means submit to your husbands as to the Lord. . . . For husbands, this means love your wives, just as Christ loved the church. He gave up his life for her . . ." (vv. 21–22, 25).

Did you notice what he did there? He begins with "submit to *one another* out of reverence for Christ" (emphasis added). The wife doesn't just submit to the husband, the husband also submits to the wife. How do we know this? Well, first of all because it says so in black-and-white, but also because he says husbands are to love their wives like Jesus loves the church and gave up his life for her. And what does that look like?

> You must have the same attitude that Christ Jesus had. Though he was God, he did not think of equality with God as something to cling to. Instead, he gave up his divine privileges; he took the humble position of a slave and was born as a human being. When he appeared in human form, he humbled himself in obedience to God and died a criminal's death on a cross. (Phil. 2:5–8)

It really begs the question: If loving your wife the way Jesus loved the church means laying down all of your privileges to the point of death, who is called to the greater act of submission?

So what's the point of inferring all this in his letter to Titus? Paul is giving larger instructions for family life because, as we learned yesterday, people are watching. Paul is calling us to "promote the kind of living that reflects wholesome teaching" (Titus 2:1). And in a culture that lives under the curse of the times then and now, teaching the good news of Jesus Christ means that the times are changing.

### The Prayer

Jesus, the good news today is that you are breaking the curse. Break it in me so my life can be a part of breaking it in others. Amen.

### The Question

- Where do you still need to have the mind of Christ so that you can reflect wholesome teaching?

# A Different Time (Part Two)

# 25

TITUS 2:9–10 | Slaves must always obey their masters and do their best to please them. They must not talk back or steal, but must show themselves to be entirely trustworthy and good. Then they will make the teaching about God our Savior attractive in every way.

### Consider This

We looked at this back in Philemon, but let's talk about slavery and Scripture again. The United States and several other countries have a dark chapter in their histories regarding slavery, and tragically certain Scripture passages were used to perpetuate this sin, including today's scripture. This was wrong.

Second, remember that context is everything. Roman Empire slavery was not the same as Confederate South slavery. In the Roman Empire slaves often received an education, were given freedom at a certain age, or would even buy and sell themselves into and out of slavery depending on their financial situation. Some have compared slavery then to a kind of "indentured servitude," but make no mistake, it was still slavery, which meant the lowest level of status for a human in the empire.

So like yesterday, it was a different time. And, remember, Paul is alluding to a bigger teaching Titus was probably familiar with: the "submit to one another out of reverence for Christ" teaching we saw yesterday. In Ephesians 5 and 6 Paul talks about husbands and wives, parents and children, and then slaves and masters:

> Slaves, obey your earthly masters with deep respect and fear. Serve them sincerely as you would serve Christ. Try to please them all the time, not just when they are watching you. As slaves of Christ, do the will of God with all your heart. Work with enthusiasm, as though you were working for the Lord rather than for

people. Remember that the Lord will reward each one of us for the good we do, whether we are slaves or free.

Masters, treat your slaves in the same way. Don't threaten them; remember, you both have the same Master in heaven, and he has no favorites. (Eph. 6:5–9)

We could stop here and tie this off with a good word about how we submit to and treat each other. But it's interesting that of all the relationship models Paul could have used to call us to be like Christ, he chose the lowest status of slavery. Why? Because that's what Jesus did. Let's again check out what Paul also says in Philippians 2:5–8:

You must have the same attitude that Christ Jesus had. Though he was God, he did not think of equality with God as something to cling to. Instead, he gave up his divine privileges; he took the humble position of a slave and was born as a human being. When he appeared in human form, he humbled himself in obedience to God and died a criminal's death on a cross.

Jesus gave up his will, desires, rights, and entitlements and submitted to taking the humble position of a slave [and dying] a criminal's death on a cross.

Now watch this:

- Romans 1:1: "This letter is from Paul, a slave of Christ Jesus."
- 2 Peter 1:1: "This letter is from Simon Peter, a slave and apostle of Jesus Christ."

- Jude 1:1: "This letter is from Jude, a slave of Jesus Christ."
- James 1:1: "This letter is from James, a slave of God and of the Lord Jesus Christ."

Each of these Jesus followers first identify themselves as slaves. In the Roman Empire, a slave's status up or down was based on their relationship with their master. My friend and New Testament scholar Ruth Anne Reese points out that by using the title of "slave," they are publicly declaring they are owned by Jesus Christ.[13]

The reason for all this slave talk in the New Testament is because we are called to be slaves of the One who became like a slave. That's the upside down of the first becoming last / love others as Jesus loved us / lay down your life / kingdom on earth as it is in heaven.

In Romans 6:16 Paul writes: "Don't you realize that you become the slave of whatever you choose to obey? You can be a slave to sin, which leads to death, or you can choose to obey God, which leads to righteous living."

It may have been a different time, but it's still the same story today: we're all going to be a slave to something . . . or Someone.

### The Prayer

Through the power of the Holy Spirit, let me be a slave of Jesus Christ by giving up my will, desires, rights, and

---

13.  Ruth Ann Reese, "Jude, James, 2 Peter" class lecture notes, Asbury Theological Seminary, Spring semester, 2007.

entitlements so that my life will make the teaching about God our Savior attractive in every way. Amen.

### The Question

- Where in your life, right now, can you submit like Christ to the form of a slave for the sake of the gospel?

# Not Yet or Right Now? | 26

TITUS 2:11–15 | For the grace of God has been revealed, bringing salvation to all people. And we are instructed to turn from godless living and sinful pleasures. We should live in this evil world with wisdom, righteousness, and devotion to God, while we look forward with hope to that wonderful day when the glory of our great God and Savior, Jesus Christ, will be revealed. He gave his life to free us from every kind of sin, to cleanse us, and to make us his very own people, totally committed to doing good deeds.

You must teach these things and encourage the believers to do them. You have the authority to correct them when necessary, so don't let anyone disregard what you say.

### Consider This

I've heard the Bible described as the acrostic B.I.B.L.E. for Basic Instructions Before Leaving Earth. I don't agree with that one because if we take Titus as an example of the whole

New Testament (which it is), the Bible is showing us how to prepare for Jesus to come back to earth, not for us to leave. Consider today's text: "We should live in this evil world with wisdom, righteousness, and devotion to God, while we look forward with hope to that wonderful day when the glory of our great God and Savior, Jesus Christ, will be revealed" (vv. 12–13).

A lot—and I mean a lot—of anxiety has been spent on when Jesus will return and what that will look like. But here Paul uses the word *hope*. That tells us that Jesus' second coming is a good thing. Why? Because the return of Jesus means it's all over: no more cancer or mental illness; no more #MeToo or school shootings; no more dictators or refugees; no more Twitter trolling and shaming; no more abuse or racism or addiction or sex slave trade or discrimination or unwanted children . . . you get the idea.

Yes, there is hope that when Jesus returns all this darkness will turn to light. But look carefully at how today's text starts: "For the grace of God has been revealed, bringing salvation to all people" (v. 11).

Do you see it? The salvation that comes through Jesus Christ has been revealed and it will be revealed. That's the tension we call the "already/not yet" because his kingdom is already here, but it has not yet been fully realized. The grace of God has been revealed by Jesus' birth, life, death, resurrection, ascension, and sending of the Holy Spirit—and it will be revealed when he returns.

Jesus' return is the only part of the story we're still waiting for, just like Paul was when he wrote this letter to Titus. It's why the New Testament calls us to live like the not yet is right now. Our waiting for that day is active by sharing the good news of salvation through Jesus Christ and resisting evil and injustice. It is living "in this evil world with wisdom, righteousness, and devotion to God" (v. 12). In other words, these are not the instructions for leaving earth, but the hope of the kingdom on earth as it is in heaven.

### The Prayer

Jesus, let your Holy Spirit show me where the "not yet" can be the "right now" and help me reveal the light of your hope into the dark places I see around me. Amen.

### The Question

- How do you look forward with this kind of hope while living in this world now?

# Take My Hand

## 27

TITUS 3:1–8 | Remind the believers to submit to the government and its officers. They should be obedient, always ready to do what is good. They must not slander anyone and must avoid quarreling. Instead, they should be gentle and show true humility to everyone.

Once we, too, were foolish and disobedient. We were misled and became slaves to many lusts and pleasures. Our lives were full of evil and envy, and we hated each other. But—

> When God our Savior revealed his kindness and love, he saved us, not because of the righteous things we had done, but because of his mercy. He washed away our sins, giving us a new birth and new life through the Holy Spirit. He generously poured out the Spirit upon us through Jesus Christ our Savior. Because of his grace he made us right in his sight and gave us confidence that we will inherit eternal life.

This is a trustworthy saying, and I want you to insist on these teachings so that all who trust in God will devote themselves to doing good. These teachings are good and beneficial for everyone.

### Consider This

It always starts with a "No!" or "That's mine!" or the ubiquitous "Don't touch me!" Then the voices get louder, louder, louder, until that split second of silence that drags out as a decision to cross the point of no return is weighed, and then, the scream. And then another.

As they run into where we are, we already know one of them drew first blood, but we don't know who because they're going to blame the other. A pinch, a scratch, a punch. Words have become an act of violence, and I'm ready to send everyone to their room with no dinner.

But my wife (a.k.a. the cool and calm one) takes over. Judgments are made and consequences are doled out. Then she takes each daughter by the hand, turns it over, and makes the sign of the cross in their palm. "Our hands can be used to hurt," she says, "or they can be used to help. Let's have Jesus' hands next time."

We're about to cross the point of no return with Titus, into the dark forest where no one is supposed to go: religion and politics. We're not supposed to talk about them in polite company or at the Thanksgiving table, but it's pretty much all we talk and tweet about these days.

And full disclosure: I live in a country that is darkly divided politically, and I serve in a denomination that is just as divided theologically. But religion and politics is right where Paul charges into without hesitation, and so will we.

I want to walk through this forest carefully because there is a safe passage through this Scripture passage, but it means we're going to have to take a path we're not used to. We're going to spend the next four days on this one text, looking at it from different sides. But trust me, we'll get through to the other side. To make sure we take the best first turn, we're starting with verse 2 instead of 1: "They must not slander anyone and must avoid quarreling. Instead, they should be gentle and show true humility to everyone."

Let's read that again, because Paul takes this first step in verse 1 by saying, "Remind the believers." There is zero ambiguity in what Paul says here; no need for commentary, scholars, or interpretation for this word between you and me. So let's go slowly word by word: Must not slander. Must avoid quarreling. Be gentle. Show humility. To everyone.

To. Every. One.

We're starting here because any talk about religion and politics can turn our words into acts of violence, and then we blame the other. So place your hand over your mouth, make the sign of the cross, and remember: your words can be used to hurt or to help. Let's have Jesus' words next time.

### The Prayer

Jesus, through your prophet Isaiah you said, "For I am the LORD your God who takes hold of your right hand and says to you, Do not fear; I will help you" (Isa. 41:13 NIV). Take my hand. I believe this. Help my unbelief. Amen.

### The Question

- Can you place your hand over your mouth until your words can be used to help and not hurt?

# 28 Following the Leader

TITUS 3:1–3 | Remind the believers to submit to the government and its officers. They should be obedient, always ready to do what is good. They must not slander anyone and must avoid quarreling. Instead, they should be gentle and show true humility to everyone.

Once we, too, were foolish and disobedient. We were misled and became slaves to many lusts and pleasures. Our lives were full of evil and envy, and we hated each other.

### Consider This

My junior year of college in 1992 was the first time I could vote for the president of the United States. It was also the first time ever my dad could vote for his leader. As a previous green card holder he could not vote in federal elections, but now he was a US citizen. So we went to the polling place together and my mom took pictures of:

The two of us signing in.

Getting our ballot.

Going behind the little partition.

Putting our ballot in the box.

As soon as we walked out the door, my father asked, "Son, who did you vote for?" We cancelled each other out, and he wasn't happy. Mom didn't get a picture of that. "Not my president," would become a common refrain between us.

"Remind the believers to submit to the government and its officers. They should be obedient, always ready to do what is good." I read this text as a citizen of the United States where we celebrate the "peaceful transfer of power" and the phrase "submit to the government" can be safely championed or ignored based on which party is in power.

N. T. Wright reminds us that in a fallen society, before Jesus returns, we need some sort of civic order: "[All] societies need some regulation, some ordering, some structure of authority

. . . and this ordering is no use unless everyone is, at least in principle, signed up to it."[14] A world without civic services, the ability to call 9-1-1, and laws to protect freedom and justice would be a world of chaos for a God who is a God of order. So, yes, government and its officers is necessary. But . . .

But what about my dad who was voting as an immigrant from Iraq, where he grew up in a time when his dear leader was chosen for him? How does "submit to the government and its officers" translate when Saddam Hussain is your government? Or Communists? Or Hitler?

What do we do with Martin Luther King Jr.? He didn't submit. If he had, then his dream would have been a nightmare. Neither did the frontmen of the Revolutionary War. If they had followed this scripture in the same way, there would be no fireworks on the 4th of July. Were they wrong?

What's going on when Paul writes this here (and in Romans)? Some scholars say Paul drops this line to protect the fragile minority of persecuted Christians in the midst of the anti-Christian Roman Empire. Submit to stay under the radar, so to speak. There is some validity to this, but that can't be the whole story.

If this statement from Paul is absolute, then the whole story of the Bible is frustratingly inconsistent with it. First of all, Paul says this kind of stuff from prison because he is not submitting to the government and so they eventually kill him. If this statement is absolute then consider:

---

14. N. T. Wright, "The Letter to the Romans: Introduction, Commentary, and Reflection" in *The New Interpreter's Bible* (Nashville, TN: Abingdon Press, 2002), 722.

- Midwives should have submitted to Pharaoh and killed all the Hebrew babies, including Moses.
- Moses should have submitted to Pharaoh and just gone back to work.
- Rahab should have submitted to the king of Jericho and turned over the Israelite spies.
- Nathan should have submitted to King David and not called him out on his adultery with Bathsheba.
- Daniel should have submitted to King Darius and not been thrown in the lions' den.
- Shadrach, Meshach, and Abednego should have submitted to King Nebuchadnezzar and not been thrown in the furnace.
- John the Baptist should have submitted to Herod and not lost his head.
- Jesus should have submitted to Pontius Pilate and not been crucified.
- John should have submitted to Caesar and not been imprisoned on Patmos.

So what is really going on here? What is the takeaway for us, and how do we put this text in its proper place? We want it to be a black-and-white statement, but it isn't. Especially when there are more non-submission stories in the Bible than submission ones.

There's confusion and danger here, but here's a good place to start regarding following the leader: "submit to one another out of reverence for Christ" (Eph. 5:21).

### The Prayer

Jesus, I submit to you as my leader, knowing you will lead me along the right road. Amen.

### The Question

- What are your thoughts or concerns about politics and religion as we go down this road?

# 29 Jesus Is Lord. Caesar Is Not. Unless . . .

TITUS 3:1–3 | Remind the believers to submit to the government and its officers. They should be obedient, always ready to do what is good. They must not slander anyone and must avoid quarreling. Instead, they should be gentle and show true humility to everyone.

Once we, too, were foolish and disobedient. We were misled and became slaves to many lusts and pleasures. Our lives were full of evil and envy, and we hated each other.

### Consider This

My mom saw President Kennedy speak in Houston the night before he was assassinated. I saw President Bush give a surprise campaign speech at a honky-tonk in college. We have a competition going between us of who has seen the most presidents in person, and I'm currently ahead 5–4.

But one day when we were comparing scores, my granny trumped us both. For the first time she revealed that when she was nine years old President Warren G. Harding held her up before a crowd of people. Her father ran the local railroad station and knew Harding would be making a campaign stop, so he brought his little girl to meet the president.

"How come you've never told us that?" we asked stunned. "How many people can say they've been held by a president!"

"I never told anyone," she said, "because he just wasn't a real good president."

If I listed off all the presidents I've seen and why and who I've voted for (I'm not), then half of you would feel we could get along and the other half would probably quit reading. We all have pretty strong feelings about this, which makes for a confusing witness because when our candidate is in power, we like to champion Paul's admonition to "submit to the government and its officers." But when it's the other party we easily and quickly shift to "resist the government and its officers."

The earliest Christians mixed politics and religion by declaring, "Jesus is Lord!" which also meant, "Caesar is not!" But let's be honest and confess that for many of us today the temptation and tendency is to say, "Jesus is Lord, Caesar is not . . . unless it's my Caesar."

We're still looking at this admonition from Paul to Titus to "Remind the believers to submit to the government and its officers. They should be obedient, always ready to do what is good," and the struggle to understand why Paul would say this if the Bible is full of people (including himself) who didn't submit.

I think the key is found in the next verse: "They should be obedient, always ready to *do what is good*" (v. 1, emphasis added).

In another letter, Paul takes doing good further:

> I urge you, first of all, to pray for all people. Ask God to help them; intercede on their behalf, and give thanks for them. Pray this way for kings and all who are in authority so that we can live peaceful and quiet lives marked by godliness and dignity. (1 Tim. 2:1–2)

Context is everything, so here's the deal: Paul is writing to a fringe community. I think Paul calls for submission to governing authorities not because they're in line with God, but because it is part of his readers' witness. It sets Jesus' followers up as a contrast to other rebelling fringe communities. If they're just another group rebelling against Caesar, then they're no different. Peaceful submission makes their life stick out for the reign of God, and that is doing good.

So what does doing good look like in a "Jesus is Lord, Caesar is not . . . unless it's my Caesar" culture? Here's a test: If we're more excited and spend more time talking about who we voted for than about Jesus and his kingdom, then Caesar is our lord. If we're spending more energy evangelizing what our candidate promises than what Jesus has already done, we've lost our witness (and maybe our soul).

The urge to make any Caesar more than they are is a temptation of the church, but as Paul continues in his letter to Timothy: "There is one God and one Mediator who can reconcile God and humanity—the man Christ Jesus. He gave his life to purchase freedom for everyone" (1 Tim. 2:5–6).

Because Jesus is Lord, Caesar is not. Period.

### The Prayer

Jesus, I pray for all people, and intercede especially for our leaders. I pray that we could live peaceful and quiet lives marked by godliness and dignity, because you are Lord. Caesar is not. And I am not. Amen.

### The Question

- Do you find you give more time and energy to what your candidate promises than what Jesus has already done? I know I have. Let's repent.

# No Salvation without Representation

# 30

TITUS 3:1–3 | Remind the believers to submit to the government and its officers. They should be obedient, always ready to do what is good. They must not slander anyone and must avoid quarreling. Instead, they should be gentle and show true humility to everyone.

Once we, too, were foolish and disobedient. We were misled and became slaves to many lusts and pleasures. Our lives were full of evil and envy, and we hated each other.

### Consider This

There is a statue of Francis Asbury, the first Methodist bishop to America, tucked away off 16th and Mt. Pleasant in Washington DC. It was dedicated by President Calvin Coolidge on October 15, 1924, to great fanfare as the "fifteenth rider to Washington." The previous fourteen statues were of generals who won wars, but Asbury was a preacher who saved souls.

"There are only two main theories of government in the world," Coolidge said, "One rests on righteousness, the other rests on force."[15]

It was at this statue on election day ninety-two years later (2016) that a few of us knelt down and prayed for how God's people would respond regardless of who won: "We are at the center of power in the world and we say that's not going to cut it," one friend prayed, "We don't blame our officials, because they reflect and represent us."

To represent means to speak for or to depict or embody, and there's something to consider in today's text about what or who we're speaking for or embodying in a world of mixed politics and religion.

---

15. Calvin Coolidge, reprinted in *The Dedicatory Address of Calvin Coolidge at the Equestrian Statue of Francis Asbury* (Franklin, TN: Seedbed, 2016).

Listen to how Paul contrasts a reflection after he calls Titus to submit to the governing authorities: "They should be gentle and show true humility to everyone. Once we, too, were foolish and disobedient. We were misled and became slaves to many lusts and pleasures. Our lives were full of evil and envy, and we hated each other" (vv. 2–3).

Gentle and humble versus evil, envious, and hateful toward each other. Are we reflecting our elected officials, or are they reflecting us? To answer that, let's go to the place in Scripture crazier than Paul talking about politics and religion: the book of Revelation and the infamous number 666.

In Revelation 13 the apostle John warns his readers not to take the "mark of the beast" because:

> He required everyone—small and great, rich and poor, free and slave—to be given a mark on the right hand or on the forehead. And no one could buy or sell anything without that mark, which was either the name of the beast or the number representing his name. Wisdom is needed here. Let the one with understanding solve the meaning of the number of the beast, for it is the number of a man. His number is 666. (vv. 16–18)

In his seminal study on Revelation, the late great New Testament scholar Robert Mulholland showed how Jewish writers like John used numbers as a form of code. Remember, John is imprisoned for not submitting to the Roman Empire and he's writing a letter under the radar warning and encouraging other Jewish Christians in the empire. Biblical Hebrew did not have numerals but instead used different letters to represent numbers, and the number 666 in Hebrew letters spelled out "Caesar Nero."[16]

John is telling his readers not to take the mark—the representation—of Caesar. He's telling them not to submit to him. And what is that mark? John says the representation of Caesar is his name, which means his nature and character: power, wealth, control. And where is that mark of representation? The hand and forehead. Now watch this because it's really cool:

In Deuteronomy 11:18 God says, "Fix these words of mine in your hearts and minds; tie them as symbols on your hands and bind them on your foreheads" (NIV). Mulholland points out that in the Hebrew mind-set, the forehead represented your worldview and the hand represented your actions based on that worldview.[17]

Do you see it? God says to let his Word be your worldview and let his Word dictate your actions. Through John, God is warning us not to take on the character of the governing authorities as our worldview or let them dictate our actions. Don't represent them.

So how do we represent his Word? If you thought that was cool, watch this: John writes in his gospel that the "Word became human and made his home among us" (John 1:14). The mark of Christ on the forehead is found in the crown of thorns. The mark of Christ on the hand is the nails of the cross.

---

16. M. Robert Mulholland, *Revelation: Holy Living in an Unholy World* (Grand Rapids, MI: Francis Asbury Press, 1990), 238.
17. Mulholland, 237.

Let's put this in black-and-white language. We can either have the worldview and actions of our favorite politician or political party, or we can have the worldview and actions of Jesus, who as Paul says in Philippians 2:5–11:

> Though he was God, he did not think of equality with God as something to cling to. Instead, he gave up his divine privileges; he took the humble position of a slave and was born as a human being. When he appeared in human form, he humbled himself in obedience to God and died a criminal's death on a cross. Therefore, God elevated him to the place of highest honor and gave him the name above all other names, that at the name of Jesus every knee should bow, in heaven and on earth and under the earth, and every tongue declare that Jesus Christ is Lord, to the glory of God the Father.

There are only two main theories of government in the world. One rests on righteousness, the other rests on force. One is Christ, the other is Caesar. And as President Coolidge went on to say at the Asbury dedication, "Christ spent no time in the antechamber of Caesar."[18]

In other words, it does not matter whether Pharaoh, emperor, führer, dictator, dear leader, your majesty, prime minister, or president sits in the seat of political power, we are to only represent the Lamb of God who sits upon the throne.

---

18. Calvin Coolidge, reprinted in *The Dedicatory Address of Calvin Coolidge at the Equestrian Statue of Francis Asbury* (Franklin, TN: Seedbed, 2016).

### The Prayer
Jesus, you are Lord. My Caesar is not. Amen.

### The Question
· Does what you post in your social media feed and what you let disciple you through the news, talk radio, and podcasts cause you to represent your favorite Caesar or Jesus?

# 31 The Politics of Jesus

TITUS 3:1–7 | Remind the believers to submit to the government and its officers. They should be obedient, always ready to do what is good. They must not slander anyone and must avoid quarreling. Instead, they should be gentle and show true humility to everyone.

Once we, too, were foolish and disobedient. We were misled and became slaves to many lusts and pleasures. Our lives were full of evil and envy, and we hated each other. But—

> When God our Savior revealed his kindness and love, he saved us, not because of the righteous things we had done, but because of his mercy. He washed away our sins, giving us a new birth and new life through the Holy Spirit. He generously poured out the Spirit upon us through Jesus Christ our Savior. Because of his grace he made us right in his sight and gave us confidence that we will inherit eternal life.

### Consider This

Recently I've come to realize that when some people don't appreciate me discussing politics, it may be because they feel that Jesus is challenging their politics.

But everything about Jesus is political. His birth was political because King Herod was so narcissistic and insecure he ordered babies killed so that Jesus wouldn't take his throne. And his death was political because as Jesus rode a donkey into Jerusalem from the east, Pontius Pilate rode a war horse in from the west. Both Herod and Pilate were the representatives and reflection of Caesar, and Jesus challenged their politics.

And that's what Paul is doing with us in today's text. We've been looking at what Paul means by "submit to the government and its officers." Remember, Paul is talking about government officers in the Roman Empire, so they're representatives and reflections of Caesar. And though he says submit, he's been secretly subverting them in plain sight this whole time.

Remember back to the end of chapter 2, right before Paul turns political, he says,

> [We] look forward with hope to that wonderful day when the glory of our great God and Savior, Jesus Christ, will be revealed. He gave his life to free us from every kind of sin, to cleanse us, and to make us his very own people . . . (Titus 2:13–14)

Then right after he talks about submitting to the government he says,

> But—When God our Savior revealed his kindness and love, he saved us, not because of the righteous things we had done, but because of his mercy. He washed away our sins, giving us a new birth and new life through the Holy Spirit. He generously poured out the Spirit upon us through Jesus Christ our Savior. Because of his grace he made us right in his sight and gave us confidence that we will inherit eternal life. (3:4–7)

Three times in those passages Paul calls Jesus "Savior," which N. T. Wright points out is the title the Romans used for Caesar because, "Caesar claimed to have rescued, or 'saved,' the world from chaos, war and anarchy."[19] In fact, the Roman coin Jesus held when he said, "give to Caesar what belongs to Caesar, and give to God what belongs to God" (Matt. 22:21) had an image of the emperor with the inscription: Augustus Tiberius, Son of the Divine and High Priest.

Do you see what Paul did there? He sandwiched submit to Caesar in between the story of how Jesus, the Son of God and our High Priest, is the One who really rescued the world from the chaos of sin. Our hope is not in the work of Caesar but in the victory of the cross and the return of Christ.

But it is not just the past and future works of Jesus that subvert the Caesars of history, it is also the present. In another letter, Paul writes that God our Savior

---

19. N. T. Wright, *Paul for Everyone: The Pastoral Letters of 1 and 2 Timothy, and Titus* (Westminster: John Knox Press, Kindle Edition), 141.

raised Christ from the dead and seated him in the place of honor at God's right hand in the heavenly realms. Now he is far above any ruler or authority or power or leader or anything else—not only in this world but also in the world to come. God has put all things under the authority of Christ and has made him head over all things for the benefit of the church. (Eph. 1:20–22)

As I write this, today is Ascension Day, a day most of us don't think about but is just as important as Christmas, Epiphany, Lent, Easter, Pentecost, and Advent. We know what it means to celebrate Jesus' birth, death, resurrection, and return, but on Ascension Day we the celebrate that right now as you read this Jesus Christ is sitting on the throne of heaven and earth. Jesus' ascension means that Jesus is Lord over my Caesar and your Caesar right now, not just when he comes back in final victory.

And it gets better because in another letter Paul says, "Christ Jesus who died—more than that, who was raised to life—is at the right hand of God and is also interceding for us" (Rom. 8:34 NIV). So not only is Jesus Lord over Caesar, he's praying for us right now in the midst of this fallen empire.

By putting Caesar and his representatives between the works of the Savior, Paul is saying that we're not living in Caesar's story, Caesar is living in Jesus' story. And as we've already seen, the more we embody Caesar's life and character, the less we proclaim the reign of Christ.

Steve Seamands writes that "whenever we fail to proclaim the ascended Christ, enthroned and exalted, something else—our personal agendas, the world's agendas, the church's agendas—moves in to fill the vacuum. Mark it down: when we fail to exalt and enthrone Jesus, something or someone else inevitably assumes the throne."[20]

So maybe when we preach about Jesus we are hearing about politics, just not ours.

### The Prayer

Jesus, you're sitting at the Father's right hand praying for me and the world right now. May my prayers for your kingdom on earth as it is heaven match yours. Amen.

### The Question

- Where has something or someone else assumed the throne in your life?

# 32 It's a Trap

TITUS 3:9–11 | Do not get involved in foolish discussions about spiritual pedigrees or in quarrels and fights about obedience to Jewish laws. These things are useless and a waste of time. If people are causing divisions among you, give a first and second warning. After that, have nothing more to do with them. For people like that have turned away from the truth, and their own sins condemn them.

---

20. Stephen Seamands, *Give Them Christ: Preaching His Incarnation, Crucifixion, Resurrection, Ascension and Return* (Downers Grove, IL: InterVarsity Press, 2012), 141.

### Consider This

Mark 12 tells the story of two different groups working together to get Jesus arrested. Some Pharisees (the religion team) and some supporters of Herod (the political team) ask Jesus if it is okay for Jews to pay taxes to Caesar.

As we saw yesterday, the coin used to pay the tax had an image of Caesar on it that read "Son of the Divine and High Priest." Under Jewish law the image of Caesar was a carved image—an idol—and so was not to be touched. But under Roman law, the tax had to be paid.

In his iconic response, Jesus takes the coin and says, "'Whose image is this? And whose inscription?' 'Caesar's,' they replied. Then Jesus said to them, 'Give back to Caesar what is Caesar's and to God what is God's.' And they were amazed at him" (Mark 12:16–17 NIV).

His answer amazed them because their question was a trap. If Jesus said yes then he'd be breaking Jewish law and could lose his crowd of followers. If he said no then he'd be breaking Roman law and arrested. Both the religious side and the political side were saying, "You're either with us or against us."

The most accepted interpretation and application of this story is that Jesus was saying, "Be a good citizen and a good church member. Pay your taxes, but also pay your tithe." But what is so amazing about that?

I once met a rabbi who said this story is really Jesus riffing on a popular rabbinic teaching question that went something like, "Whose image is on humanity?" And the answer is, "God's."

The coin bears the image of a fake god. But humanity bears the image of the Trinity. So imagine Jesus separating church and state by saying, "Whose image is on the coin? And whose image is on humanity? Well then give back to Caesar what is Caesar's and give back to God what is God's." He walked out of their trap by not falling for the argument between religion and politics.

In today's text, Paul moves his discussion of religion and politics with the admonition to "not get involved in foolish discussions," or get into "quarrels and fights" because they are "useless and a waste of time." Then he ups the stakes by saying if people do get into those kinds of fights to "have nothing more to do with them."

This follows his own testimony from yesterday's text that, "Our lives were full of evil and envy, and we hated each other" (Titus 3:3). Paul is warning us about the you're either with us or against us trap of religion and politics many of us fall into today in our current cultural, political, and denominational realities.

The issue is not a difference of opinion. We all come from very different theological backgrounds, denominational traditions, and varying experiences. Our religion wasn't even crawling before these differences came up (see Acts 15).

The issue is how we talk to one another and treat each other in the midst of these differences. And nowhere is that a more dangerous issue than online. Lost in the tweets and comments section are our tone, facial expressions, and body language—those non-verbal cues that make up almost 90 percent of effective communication. This leaves us with only the words we use, which is *really* important since the words we say have the power of life and death (see Proverbs 18:21).

The issue we're struggling with is not debate but argument. There is a difference between defending the faith and destroying your opponent; between having the right words and warring to be right. A rebuke is not the same as a take-down. Name-calling is not the same as "in the name of Jesus."

Scripture has lots to say about how to deal with each other in our disagreements, and some examples include:

- 2 Timothy 2:24: "A servant of the Lord must not quarrel but must be kind to everyone, be able to teach, and be patient with difficult people."
- Titus 3:2: "[Believers] must not slander anyone and must avoid quarreling. Instead, they should be gentle and show true humility to everyone."
- James 3:9–10 (NIV): "With the tongue we praise our Lord and Father, and with it we curse human beings, who have been made in God's likeness. Out of the same mouth come praise and cursing. My brothers and sisters, this should not be."
- Titus 3:10: "If people are causing divisions among you, give a first and second warning. After that, have nothing more to do with them."
- Ephesians 4:29: "Do not use foul or abusive language. Let everything you say be good and helpful, so that your words will be an encouragement to those who hear them."

And, of course, all the love in 1 Corinthians 13 can't be read apart from the warnings in chapter 12. This last one is most important because we are in a very angry era, so let's just call it what it is: sin. Satan is using social media and 24-hour news commentary to steal, kill, and destroy.

It's a trap.

True love is a subversive counter-attack, but loses all its power if we're just attacking each other. We need to always be praying for the Holy Spirit to help us confront without being confrontational and to not be conformed by the ways of the Twitter world. This is the difference between bearing the image of Caesar and bearing the image of the Trinity.

We can easily end up the people Paul says "have turned away from the truth, and their own sins condemn them" (Titus 3:11). But thankfully Paul gives us another option—a Jesus option—to walk out of the trap: "Live wisely among those who are not believers, and make the most of every opportunity. Let your conversation be gracious and attractive so that you will have the right response for everyone" (Col. 4:5–6).

Let today's Caesars and their followers have all the nasty conflict and conversation. Instead let's give to each other, who are made in God's image, what is God's.

### *The Prayer*

Jesus, cleanse us from the scourge of insult and incivility of our nation's discourse. Govern our hearts, our minds, and our words that we would no longer contribute to the discord but become sowers of your peace and of your Word. Awaken us again to your high calling to be the salt of the earth and the light of the world. Amen.[21]

### The Question

- Where do you see the traps laid before you, and where have you fallen in? Let's confess them and repent.

# All Politics Is Local

# 33

TITUS 3:12–15 | I am planning to send either Artemas or Tychicus to you. As soon as one of them arrives, do your best to meet me at Nicopolis, for I have decided to stay there for the winter. Do everything you can to help Zenas the lawyer and Apollos with their trip. See that they are given everything they need. Our people must learn to do good by meeting the urgent needs of others; then they will not be unproductive.

Everybody here sends greetings. Please give my greetings to the believers—all who love us.

May God's grace be with you all.

### Consider This

We're back where we started with Titus: getting personal. Paul wrote this letter for a local audience, so he said some

---

21. Taken from the election day prayers at the Francis Asbury statue in Washington DC.

tougher things. Personal conversations carry more weight, and sometimes we don't like what people say. We call it someone "stepping on our toes," which means what they've said is upsetting because it gets into something personal. This happens in almost all relationships (and sermons) at some point.

Pastor Louie Giglio once told a crowd he was going to step on their toes with his sermon, but he wanted to illustrate how he would do it. He called someone on stage and said he was going to physically step on their toes. As he did, he also put his arms around them. What that means, Louie said, was that if I'm close enough to step on your toes I'm also close enough to embrace you.[22]

At the end of this letter Paul lists some seemingly unimportant names with some instructions that don't mean anything to us. A lot of these letters end like this and we usually skip them, but they meant something to Paul. And in the middle of listing his itinerary he drops: "Our people must learn to do good by meeting the urgent needs of others; then they will not be unproductive" (v. 14).

Maybe not the nicest way he could have encouraged them, but it's said in the same spirit as what he wrote earlier in the letter: "You must teach these things and encourage the believers to do them. You have the authority to correct them when necessary, so don't let anyone disregard what you say" (2:15).

---

22. This story came from my friend Drew Causey who heard Louie Giglio speak at the Big Stuff Camp in Panama City Beach, 1999.

In other words, he and Titus have the authority to step on toes, but only because they're close enough to embrace. Paul has invested himself in Titus and the other folks he names. These tough letters are rooted in deep relationship and show us we can give and receive challenging words if they are rooted in deep love.

Consider the Pharisees. They are the ubiquitous bad guys of the Gospels. Jesus always railed against these religious leaders for playing politics. We're warned never to be one and yet we often give the title to other religious people we don't agree with.

But Jesus loved the Pharisees. Of all the Jewish groups, they were the ones he probably most identified with theologically. They were the Law-keepers, they just couldn't see he was the Law (see Matthew 5:17). That's why he was so frustrated with them and stepped on their toes all the time: because his authority to correct them came from a place of embrace. Don't believe me? Look at the story of Jesus and Nicodemus in John 3.

Nicodemus was a Pharisee who had reached a point of holy discontent. So he seeks out Jesus in the cover of darkness and Jesus steps on his toes: "You are a respected Jewish teacher, and yet you don't understand these things?" (John 3:10).

But here's something you may never have noticed: It is during their conversation that Jesus says, "For God so loved the world that he gave his only Son, so that everyone who believes in him will not perish but have eternal life" (John 3:16). The most trumpet-blasted, well-known, publicly professed scripture in human history. But it wasn't said in a sermon to the crowds. Jesus said it to Nicodemus, one-on-one in a middle-of-the-night conversation. Jesus just stepped on his toes, but now he was embracing him. And Nicodemus must have embraced a relationship with Jesus, because when Jesus is being taken down from the cross, one of the people helping embalm his body is Nicodemus. And then Nicodemus must have built a relationship and told John 3:16 to someone else, because now we all know it.

If you take nothing else away from this series, take this: there is a time for words that are challenging, words that defend the faith, and words that take a stand. But they must be words rooted in an embrace of the love that comes from a deep relationship with Jesus and a deep relationship with others.

In his book *Shaped by the Bible*, Will Willimon says,

> The Bible is "political" in the classic sense of the word politics—the formation of a polis, the constitution of a people through a discussion of what needs are worth having, what goals are good. Thus the Bible must be read "politically," that is, it must be read from a desire to form a new people.[23]

We say we want a Holy Spirit awakening in our world, but our public posturing, online arguments, and hash-tagging is not going to cut it. Why? Because whatever God does big

---

23. William H. Willimon, *Shaped by the Bible* (Nashville, TN: Abingdon Press, 1990), 19.

he first does small—in our personal relationships and home communities meeting the urgent needs of others. So if what Willimon says is true, then Paul and Titus, and Nicodemus and John 3:16, are proof that when it comes to the gospel, all politics is local.

### The Prayer

Jesus, because you love me help me love the others closest to me like you do. Amen.

### The Question

- Where and who is your local?

# Thanks, Bro

**34**

JUDE 1–2 NIV | Jude, a servant of Jesus Christ and a brother of James,

To those who have been called, who are loved in God the Father and kept for Jesus Christ:

Mercy, peace and love be yours in abundance.

### Consider This

Jesus. He's the Son of God. The Messiah. Emmanuel. The Prince of Peace. The Word made flesh. The Lamb of God who takes away the sins of the world.

And a big brother.

Not a part of the incarnation you think about, right? What was that like? Matthew 13:35 tells us Jesus had four little brothers: James, Joseph, Simon, and Jude (or Judas). If Matthew's order is correct, that makes Jude the littlest brother. What was it like between them growing up? Did he and Jesus get along? Was Jesus a cool big brother, or did he pick on his little brother? Did they fight all the time?

We have no idea. But whatever their childhood was like, by the time Jesus publicly comes out as the Son of God and starts teaching, healing, and gaining a following, his brothers think he's crazy. Mark 3:21 says: "When his family heard what was happening, they tried to take him away. 'He's out of his mind,' they said."

Later, because of a plot to kill him, Jesus avoids Judea and comes back around the neighborhood. John 7:3–5 says: "Jesus' brothers said to him, 'Leave here and go to Judea, where your followers can see your miracles! You can't become famous if you hide like this! If you can do such wonderful things, show yourself to the world!' For even his brothers didn't believe in him."

Thanks, bros.

Even his brothers didn't believe in him. The ones who knew him the longest and probably the best, his very own flesh and blood, are mocking him in the face of death. But now here's little brother writing a letter defending his big brother (and little brother James gets a book in the New Testament too). What happened between them that changed?

Answer: the resurrection.

Though the Scripture doesn't tell us what happened, it's a safe bet the brothers saw Jesus crucified and then sometime after Easter morning they saw him alive. Then they believed in him.

Acts 1:14 has Jesus' brothers present at his ascension, and they become part of the group praying to receive the Holy Spirit at Pentecost: "They all joined together constantly in prayer, along with the women and Mary the mother of Jesus, and with his brothers" (NIV).

And as we'll see in the coming days, Jude has gone from ridicule to praise; from mocking to defending. No longer a snot but a servant of Jesus. Before we get into the letter, let's not miss Jude's transformation, because it is literally the power of Christ alive in a person.

Jude's story reminds us that not everyone close to us is going to be in the same place we are with Jesus. It may take years, even decades, of prayer before we might see the power of Christ alive in them. Jude's story also shows us that we may have a relationship with Christ, but there may be a part of our lives where we may not be ready to believe Jesus and let him be Lord.

Jude also shows us that no matter where we are, there is more and more mercy, peace, and love—because whatever their relationship before, he says in today's text that his big brother loves us and keeps us safe in his care.

### The Prayer

Jesus, where my life has mocked you, forgive me. If there is a situation or part of my life where I still have not believed in you, help me surrender to your love and care. Amen.

### The Questions

- Is there a situation or part of your life where you have still not believed in who Jesus is or what he is wanting for you? Is there a person close to you who does not believe? Pray for them right now.

# 35 Why, What, How

**JUDE 3** | Dear friends, I had been eagerly planning to write to you about the salvation we all share. But now I find that I must write about something else, urging you to defend the faith that God has entrusted once for all time to his holy people.

### Consider This

Today my three daughters are ages ten, eight, and four, which means that for almost a decade I've lived in the age of "Why, Daddy?"

"I want you to turn off the TV." "Why, Daddy?" "So you can come eat your dinner." "Why?" "So you can go to bed." "Why?" "Because you need your sleep." "Why?" And even though I said I would never do it, I often become my parents and default to the dreaded, "Because I said so."

But did you notice that in this classic daddy-daughter litany I've only told her what I want her to do. And as the debate continues I'll tell her how I want her to do it: (i.e., "Sit down, stop talking, and put food in your mouth").

But in my impatience, I often don't answer her why. If I'm a good and patient father, I explain the why: "Because you need to eat well and get sleep," which becomes "Because your body is growing and you need nutrients and rest," which becomes, "So you grow up healthy," which really is all a way of saying, "Because I love you."

The key to effective parenting (and pastoring, leadership, or just living life) is about finding the why. It's one thing to say what you want to do and how you want to do it. But why? Finding the why helps better determine the what and the how.[24]

For example: What do you do? You pray to Jesus. How? Maybe a quiet time in the morning or group liturgy at church. But why do you pray? Answer that and your prayer life will change.

Why, what, and how is the key to Jude's little letter to a small group of friends. He starts today by giving us the what: "defend the faith." In *The Message*, Eugene Peterson translates Jude's what as "to guard and cherish" the faith.

Tomorrow we'll begin to look at why we need to guard and cherish the faith. It will take us a few days to go through it, but stick with it. It's just as important today as it was then.

---

24. This idea was inspired by Simon Sinek's Ted Talk: www.ted.com/talks/simon _sinek_how_great_leaders_inspire_action.

And at the end, Jude will give us the how (hint: it's not the way you'd think).

Until then, let's prepare our hearts because, according to Jesus' little brother, defending the faith is what "God has entrusted once for all time to his holy people." That includes you and me.

### The Prayer

Jesus, give me more and more mercy, peace, and love so I can know the why, what, and how of your will. Amen.

### The Question

- If you know the what and the how you follow Jesus, could you tell another person why?

## 36 Teachers Matter

**JUDE 4 NIV** | **For certain individuals whose condemnation was written about long ago have secretly slipped in among you. They are ungodly people, who pervert the grace of our God into a license for immorality and deny Jesus Christ our only Sovereign and Lord.**

### Consider This

Before I became a pastor I was a teacher, and my first gig was full-time substitute . . . essentially, a traveling teacher. One of my first jobs was a three-month stint teaching freshmen World History. I had no idea what I was doing, and after my first week all I wanted to do was apologize to every teacher I'd ever had and then lay in the fetal position in a dark room. I was terrible.

We were studying World War I, and I just wasn't getting through. On the final test, the students regurgitated facts, but I wasn't sure they really learned anything. That is until one of the most difficult students in the class wrote, "Germany was the ants in France's pants."

I got through to one.

At the end of the semester the administration asked if I wanted to get certified and come back. I said "no thank you" because those students needed someone more qualified; someone who could get through to more than one, because teachers matter.

Yesterday we saw the what of Jude's letter: defend the faith. Today we begin to see the why: because teachers matter.

Jude says some ungodly people have "secretly slipped in among you." Remember, just like we saw in 2 John, these churches were not like the ones we have today. They were intimate gatherings of a few people who met in someone's home. Remember, it was common in these first home churches for traveling teachers to pass through. And just like John, it seems Jude was addressing the issue of traveling teachers preaching and teaching false doctrine that could be getting through to more than one.

But it wasn't just any false doctrine they were teaching, it was a big one, and the reason for the big why of this letter.

They were teaching that God's marvelous grace allows us to live immoral lives. In other words, God's grace gives us license. In other words, because of grace God will love us no matter what, so we can do whatever.

But, nope, Jude is not having it.

Jude calls out the same thing Paul addressed in Romans 6:14–16:

> . . . for you no longer live under the requirements of the law. Instead, you live under the freedom of God's grace. Well then, since God's grace has set us free from the law, does that mean we can go on sinning? Of course not! Don't you realize that you become the slave of whatever you choose to obey? You can be a slave to sin, which leads to death, or you can choose to obey God, which leads to righteous living.

And, actually, they were teaching an even bigger one: "they have denied our only Master and Lord, Jesus Christ" (Jude 4).

Again, Jude isn't having it. And, again, Paul in Romans 10:9 backs him up: "If you openly declare that Jesus is Lord and believe in your heart that God raised him from the dead, you will be saved."

(Side note: remember how John was dealing with false teachers who did not believe Jesus came in a real body, which means he couldn't rise from the dead? Yeah, probably the same brand of teachers. Are you seeing a pattern?)

Eugene Peterson calls Jude a whistleblower,[25] his letter warning churches of the real danger threatening the core of the faith, which is why Jude calls for a defense (again, hang on to the end of letter to see this in a different way).

But Jude's whistleblowing was not just for his friends. There's a reason his letter is in the canon of Scripture, and it's probably because the Holy Spirit knew the church would always need a whistleblower. I'll let N. T. Wright have the last word from his study on Jude:

> Find people today who say that God loves everyone exactly as they are, so everyone must stay exactly as they are, doing all the things they want to do, because God is so full of generosity that obviously he wants them to do that; find such people, and you've found those of whom [Jude] is writing. Find people today who say that Jesus is one religious teacher among others, one way of salvation among others, that there might well be a variety of paths up the mountain of which Jesus' path is only one, that it's important not to make exclusive claims or we'll become arrogant; find such people, and you've found those of whom [Jude] is writing.[26]

---

25. Eugene Peterson, *The Message: The Bible in Contemporary Language* (Colorado Springs, CO: NavPress, 2004), 1430.

26. N. T. Wright, *1 and 2 Peter and Jude* (InterVarsity Press, Kindle Edition), 53.

### The Prayer

Jesus, give me more and more mercy, peace, and love. Help me hold fast to your teaching and not be swayed from your truth. For the sake of the gospel, amen.

### The Question

- Who are your teachers and what are you learning?

# 37 A Big Deal

**JUDE 5A  |  So I want to remind you, though you already know these things, that Jesus first rescued the nation of Israel from Egypt . . .**

### Consider This

Hold on a second. We need to pause where we're going with this letter to make sure we don't miss something big. In a letter so short, one little line can be easy to skim over: "Jesus first rescued the nation of Israel from Egypt."

Jude is saying Jesus was there at the exodus, in the Old Testament. That's a big deal.

Now some translations say "Lord" but the earliest manuscripts said "Jesus." And Jude says he's reminding his friends of something they already know, and it starts with Jesus in the Old Testament. He's not saying anything new here. Consider John 1:1–4: "In the beginning the Word already existed. The Word was with God, and the Word was God. He existed in the beginning with God. God created everything through him, and nothing was created except through him. The Word gave life to everything that was created . . ."

Or Colossians 1:15–17:

> Christ is the visible image of the invisible God. He existed before anything was created and is supreme over all creation, for through him God created everything in the heavenly realms and on earth. He made the things we can see and the things we can't see—such as thrones, kingdoms, rulers, and authorities in the unseen world. Everything was created through him and for him. He existed before anything else, and he holds all creation together.

Or Hebrews 1:2: "through the Son [God] created the universe." God through Jesus Christ created everything.

God through Jesus Christ holds all of creation together.

That means that everyone—even the false teachers—were created by Jesus, for Jesus, and are sustained by Jesus even if they're not aware of it. (Pro tip: that's a great place to pray for unbelievers because it is the very heart of prevenient grace.)

That's a big deal.

"You search the Scriptures because you think they give you eternal life," Jesus said to the Old Testament experts in John 5:39, "But the Scriptures point to me!" As my friend Matt LeRoy says, Jesus is not only the protagonist of the New Testament, he's the author of the Old Testament.

Every major covenant in the Old Testament—the ones with Adam, Noah, Abraham, Moses, and David—were pointing to Jesus. If Jesus was there to walk God's people out of Egypt, was it also Jesus who walked with Adam and Eve in the garden? Who walked up to Jacob and wrestled him? Who walked in to the tent and spoke with Moses face-to-face like a friend? Who walked in to the furnace of fire with Shadrach, Meshach, and Abednego? Who walked into a pit and shut the mouths of a bunch of lions so they wouldn't eat Daniel?

Were you ever aware of this? It's a big deal.

Jude says he's reminding his friends of something they already know, and sometimes we need to be reminded of something we already know too. Jesus who spoke creation into existence and walked out of slavery through the desert and stood in the fire and shut the mouth of lions and wrestled with Jacob is here with us now. God through Jesus Christ is here with you. Right here, right now. Even as you read this. Jesus is walking through every fire, desert, and wrestling of faith you walk through—even if you're not aware of it.

That's a big deal.

### The Prayer

Jesus, give me more and more mercy, peace, and love. Help me to see where you are walking with me, even when I haven't been aware of it. I need you to be a big deal in my life. Amen.

### *The Question*

- Where have you seen Jesus walking with you in the past that you weren't aware of and where do you see him now?

# Dereliction of Duty

# 38

**JUDE 5–11 MSG** | I'm laying this out as clearly as I can, even though you once knew all this well enough and shouldn't need reminding. Here it is in brief: The Master saved a people out of the land of Egypt. Later he destroyed those who defected. And you know the story of the angels who didn't stick to their post, abandoning it for other, darker missions. But they are now chained and jailed in a black hole until the great Judgment Day. Sodom and Gomorrah, which went to sexual rack and ruin along with the surrounding cities that acted just like them, are another example. Burning and burning and never burning up, they serve still as a stock warning.

This is exactly the same program of these latest infiltrators: dirty sex, rule and rulers thrown out, glory dragged in the mud.

The Archangel Michael, who went to the mat with the Devil as they fought over the body of Moses, wouldn't have dared level him with a blasphemous curse, but said simply, "No you don't. God will take care of you!" But these people sneer at anything they can't understand, and by doing whatever they feel like doing—living by animal instinct only—they participate in their own destruction. I'm fed up with them! They've gone down Cain's road; they've been sucked into Balaam's error by greed; they're canceled out in Korah's rebellion.

### Consider This

When I was growing up, my father had three standard stories he would march out for almost any situation where I wasn't doing what I was supposed to be doing. One of them involved school. Whenever I would bring home a bad grade on a test or report card, I knew what was coming: the story of how he would come home from school and not eat dinner until he finished all of his homework. Sometimes he would even do extra work. His mother would beg and plead and yell for him to come eat, but education came first.

He rolled this story out every time I came up short academically, from elementary school through college. It was a form of warning and judgment, which is exactly what Jude is doing in today's text.

These Old Testament stories he rapidly fires off could each have their own entry. But the heart of the matter is that these were the standard stories rolled out by Jewish and Christian writers to show the consequences of rebellion. Many are in writings not in our Protestant Bibles (like in the book of Maccabees or Sirach), but you can find them in 2 Peter.

Jude told us the *what* of his letter (defend the faith) and now he's getting to the *why* by rolling out a well-known and well-used set of stories about rebellion and judgment, but did you notice how he used them?

I went with Eugene Peterson's translation here because of the way he defines certain aspects of how these characters came up short: Defected. Abandoning. Acted just like them (which is a form of surrender). Doing whatever they felt like doing. Greed. Rebellion.

The words he uses to describe the rebellion and judgment of false teaching are all words that show a dereliction of duty: a deliberate failure to follow orders or do what you're supposed to do.

None of the folks in these stories defended the faith, and Jude is warning what the consequences of dereliction look like. This is the start of Jude's why we should defend the faith, but before we go on there is a warning for us. We could also be the ones in dereliction of duty, deceived into going on other dark missions and sneering at what we don't understand.

So before we take these past few days with Jude and sling them like arrows at those we're certain are AWOL in the faith, it would be prudent for us to recognize that we could do the same thing, and in some ways may have already.

### The Prayer

Jesus, give me more and more mercy, peace, and love. Help me to see where I've been in rebellion to you, even if I wasn't aware of it. Forgive me and free me. Amen.

### The Question

- What does dereliction of duty mean to you in how you follow Jesus?

# 39 False Positives

**JUDE 12–16** | When these people eat with you in your fellowship meals commemorating the Lord's love, they are like dangerous reefs that can shipwreck you. They are like shameless shepherds who care only for themselves. They are like clouds blowing over the land without giving any rain. They are like trees in autumn that are doubly dead, for they bear no fruit and have been pulled up by the roots. They are like wild waves of the sea, churning up the foam of their shameful deeds. They are like wandering stars, doomed forever to blackest darkness.

Enoch, who lived in the seventh generation after Adam, prophesied about these people. He said, "Listen! The Lord is coming with countless thousands of his holy ones to execute judgment on the people of the world. He will convict every person of all the ungodly things they have done and for all the insults that ungodly sinners have spoken against him."

These people are grumblers and complainers, living only to satisfy their desires. They brag loudly about themselves, and they flatter others to get what they want.

### Consider This

Hey, Jude, we get it, false teachers are bad. But does anyone else think he's gone a bit too simile-heavy for too much of this little letter?

Did you notice there's a pattern: humans and animals (shameless shepherds), sky (clouds without rain), land (trees without fruit), sea (wild waves), and the cosmos (wandering stars doomed to darkness). These are all elements of the created order in Genesis 1 and 2, and all of creation was broken at the fall in Genesis 3. False teachers perpetuate what happened in Eden over a lie, and this still impacts everything between you and me.

That's the reason for Jude's strong warning, because being false doesn't look as obvious as we think it does. Since the beginning when Satan tempted Eve, the work of false teachers has often appeared just righteous enough that we almost can't tell the difference. And because every part of creation is infected, it can impact every part of our lives. So how do we let false teaching in? As I asked yesterday, how can we partic-ipate in it without even knowing it? The clue is in the line: "When these people eat with you in your fellowship meals commemorating the Lord's love."

Jude is talking about Holy Communion, one of the most sacred sacraments and practices of the church that form us, both individually and as a people. Jude is warning of letting false teachers and their teachings infect believers' sacred space and time.

Now remember, churches then met in more intimate home settings, and part of their practice was to share a full meal that ended with Holy Communion. In this setting traveling teachers would come through and infect the congregation. Our church culture and practices are different today, but the danger is still real. The warning for us is not so much who weekly preaches in your pulpit, but who daily speaks into your soul.

Another way to ask this is: What is your primary source of discipleship? Discipleship means you closely follow the teaching of someone, so who is that primary person or persons? In my experience, the primary source of discipleship for many people are the voices of social media, cable news, and talk radio. And if we're really honest, a good portion of that combination broadcast people who are "grumblers and complainers, living only to satisfy their desires. They brag loudly about themselves, and they flatter others to get what they want," many times while trying to sound just righteous enough.

What is the impact in our lives if our primary source of discipleship is rooted in gossip, fear-mongering, and sensationalism? It metastasizes in our souls and witness. In his introduction to Jude in *The Message* translation, Eugene Peterson says, "Our spiritual communities are as susceptible to disease as our physical bodies. But it is easier to detect whatever is wrong in our stomachs and lungs than in our worship and witness. [A] dangerous, even deadly, virus in our spiritual communities can go undetected for a long time."[27]

The same is true in our own souls. Peterson calls Jude's letter a "diagnosis" for a group of believers who "apparently didn't know anything was wrong."[28]

### The Prayer

Jesus, give me more and more mercy, peace, and love. If I'm going to be your disciple, may you be the one to disciple

---

27. Eugene Peterson, *The Message: The Bible in Contemporary Language* (Colorado Springs, CO: NavPress, 2004), 1430.
28. Ibid.

me most, through the power of your Holy Spirit and in your Word. Amen.

### The Question

- What is a primary source of your discipleship that maybe shouldn't be?

# Knowing Is Half the Battle

# 40

**JUDE 17–19 NIV** | But, dear friends, remember what the apostles of our Lord Jesus Christ foretold. They said to you, "In the last times there will be scoffers who will follow their own ungodly desires." These are the people who divide you, who follow mere natural instincts and do not have the Spirit.

### Consider This

So we've looked at the what of Jude's letter (defend the faith) and we're closing out the why (because of false teaching). But before we get to the how, there's one last reason we need to know about.

Anyone out there remember the old *G.I. Joe* cartoon series? Every episode ended with a PSA (public service announcement) for kids about things like not talking to strangers, what to do in case of a fire, or making sure to tell the truth. They always ended with the refrain: "Now you know, and knowing is half the battle."

Today Jude wants to remind us of something we should already know: that in the days after Jesus' resurrection and ascension, before he returns (which is the time we're living in), there "will be scoffers who will follow their own ungodly desires" (NIV).

The word "scoffer" here is the Greek word *empaiktes*, describing a mocking and rejection of divine authority. And the rejection of divine authority is the root of all sin when Adam and Eve looked to be fulfilled by something other than God.

In other words, they looked to something false. And when you become false, you teach false. The real endgame of false teachers comes from the false self, which is the identity and sense of worth we've created for ourselves apart from God. It's the fallen (natural) instinct we follow when we reject the Holy Spirit. In his book *The Way of the Heart*, Henri Nouwen defines the false self as compulsive:

> Compulsive is indeed the best adjective for the false self. It points to the need for ongoing and increasing affirmation. Who am I? I am the one who is liked, praised, admired, disliked, hated or despised. Whether I am a pianist, a businessman or a minister, what matters is how I am perceived by my world. If being busy is a good thing, then I must be busy. If having money is a sign of real freedom, then I must claim my money. If knowing many people proves my importance, I will have to make the necessary contacts. The compulsion

manifests itself in the lurking fear of failure and the steady urge to prevent this by gathering more of the same—more work, more money, more friends.[29]

This could apply to any of us. It's easy to get worked up over theological arguments and say, "They're wrong! They're a false teacher" while never realizing any of us could be operating out of the false self, which as disciples called to make disciples, makes any of us a false teacher.

It's a battle, and that's why we still need this letter. But maybe it's also the reason so few read, study, or preach from Jude: because either we don't know our false self and the division it's creating, or the enemy wants to keep it that way.

But now you know, and knowing is half the battle.

### The Prayer

Jesus, give me more and more mercy, peace, and love. Forgive me if I have created division out of my false self, whether that division is in my community, my family, or just in me. Free me by the power of your Holy Spirit. Amen.

### The Question

- Where do you see evidence of the false self in your life, and where do you see the possibility of the Holy Spirit?

---

29. Henri Nouwen, *The Way of the Heart: Desert Spirituality and Contemporary Ministry* (San Francisco: HarperCollins, 1981), 22–23.

# 41 Don't Get Defensive

**JUDE 20–21 MSG** | But you, dear friends, carefully build yourselves up in this most holy faith by praying in the Holy Spirit, staying right at the center of God's love, keeping your arms open and outstretched, ready for the mercy of our Master, Jesus Christ. This is the unending life, the *real* life!

### Consider This

Let's be clear: there are legitimate false teachers out there who are leading people away from the apostolic faith found in the authority of Scripture and the Apostles' and Nicene Creeds. And we've also seen the last few days how the false self and false teaching go hand in hand. We've seen the what and the why, so how do we defend the faith from false teaching?

By not getting defensive.

Think about our primary posture when someone comes against us or what we believe; it usually starts with fear and anger. Our first response is to get them before they get us: to argue, scold, politic, or even cynically ridicule. And if we're not careful, defending the faith this way can take over our lives and we become a monster to defeat a monster.

But turning to Eugene Peterson again, he says, "There is far more, of course, to living in Christian community than protecting the faith against assault or subversion. Paranoia is as unhealthy spiritually as it is mentally. The primary Christian posture is, in Jude's words, 'keeping your arms open and outstretched, ready for the mercy of our Master Jesus Christ.'"[30]

In other words, don't get defensive.

Instead of exhausting ourselves tearing arguments down, Jude calls us to build each other up in prayer and by the power of the Holy Spirit. Instead of running off to fight, he calls us to run into the center of God's love.

Jude is echoing what the apostle Paul says about the battle and the "armor of God" in Ephesians 6:10–18:

> Be strong in the Lord and in his mighty power. Put on all of God's armor so that you will be able to stand firm against all strategies of the devil. For we are not fighting against flesh-and-blood enemies, but against evil rulers and authorities of the unseen world, against mighty powers in this dark world, and against evil spirits in the heavenly places. Therefore, put on every piece of God's armor so you will be able to resist the enemy in the time of evil. Then after the battle you will still be standing firm. Stand your ground, putting on the belt of truth and the body armor of God's righteousness. For shoes, put on the peace that comes from the Good News so that you will be fully prepared. In addition to all of these, hold up the shield of faith to stop the fiery arrows of the devil. Put on salvation as your helmet, and take the sword of the Spirit, which

---

30. Eugene Peterson, *The Message: The Bible in Contemporary Language* (Colorado Springs, CO: NavPress, 2004), 1430.

> is the word of God. Pray in the Spirit at all times and on every occasion. Stay alert and be persistent in your prayers for all believers everywhere.

Instead of getting angry and vengeful toward false teachers, we're called to remember that our battle isn't really with them but with spiritual forces.

And if we pay close attention, we see that all our defensive armor is really Jesus Christ himself: truth, righteousness, peace, faith, salvation, Word. As we saw in 2 John, Jesus doesn't just speak the truth, he is Truth. He doesn't just have peace, he is Peace. He doesn't just offer salvation, he is Salvation. He doesn't just speak the word of God, he is the Word who existed in the beginning. Do you see where this is going?

Jesus Christ is our first and last line of defense. Our primary task is not getting defensive, but running into his defense. The first part of how we defend the faith has nothing to do with our position with the other person, but everything to do with our position in Christ.

So how should we interact with a person we consider a false teacher or enemy of the faith? Good question, because the battle belongs to the Lord.

### The Prayer

Jesus, give me more and more mercy, peace, and love. I put on the full armor of God, which is you, and pray that by the power of the Holy Spirit you would keep me safe and build me up. Amen.

### The Question

- Does today's text cause you to reconsider your posture toward those you see as false teachers or enemies of the faith?

# Oh Mercy

**42**

**JUDE 22–23** | And you must show mercy to those whose faith is wavering. Rescue others by snatching them from the flames of judgment. Show mercy to still others, but do so with great caution, hating the sins that contaminate their lives.

### Consider This

We made it. We're finally here. How do we actually deal with those we see as false? How do we actually defend the faith?

Show mercy. That's it.

Mercy is showing compassion or forgiveness to someone you have the ability or power to harm.

Defend with mercy. That's it.

But can we be honest and admit that defending anything in twenty-first-century America tends to show no mercy? Defending the faith looks an awful lot like defending our politics or our rights: lots of outrage, posturing, arguments, Twitter trolling, score keeping, and cynical condescension. It looks like exercising our ability to do harm, winning at all costs by decimating your opponent with shame.

But did you catch the story Jude told a few verses back about the archangel Michael fighting with Satan? They're arguing over Moses' body, and the top angel won't even shame Satan! Instead, he defends Moses saying, "The Lord rebuke you!" Put another way, "God will deal with you, not me."

A mentor once gave me the best piece of evangelism advice I've ever heard, and it also works for defending the faith: never confuse your role as a witness with the role of the Holy Spirit. Your job is simply to bear witness to Jesus. Their response is the Holy Spirit's responsibility.

Let me say that again: Never confuse your role as a witness with the role of the Holy Spirit. Your job is simply to bear witness to Jesus. Their response is the Holy Spirit's responsibility.

Remember all those folks we come in contact with that Jude dramatically described earlier as "dangerous reefs," "doubly dead," and "lost stars"? He says in verse 15 that "[God] will convict every person of all ungodly things they have done."

I'll say it again: Never confuse your role as a witness with the role of the Holy Spirit. Your job is simply to bear witness to Jesus. Their response is the Holy Spirit's responsibility.

Yes, we speak truth to power and stand up for what's right. Preach the gospel and by all means call out false teaching. But if someone is false, our job is to tell them the truth, and the truth is the person of Jesus Christ. Let Jesus deal with their reaction.

There's a difference between defending with shame and defending with mercy. To defend the faith with mercy looks like Jesus on the cross. It looks like the Sermon on the Mount. It looks like the prayer Jude opened this letter with, and the prayer we've been praying this whole time: Give us more and more mercy, peace, and love. After all, once we were enemies of God, but he showed us mercy through Jesus (see Romans 5:10).

A couple of days ago we said knowing is half the battle, and the battle is the Lord's. So now you know the other half: God will deal with them. Not you.

### The Prayer

Jesus, give me more and more mercy, peace, and love. Help me to not confuse my role as a witness with the role of the Holy Spirit. Amen.

### The Question

- How have you confused your role as a witness with the role of the Holy Spirit?

# The Formula 43

JUDE 24–25 | Now all glory to God, who is able to keep you from falling away and will bring you with great joy into his glorious presence without a single fault. All glory to him who alone is God, our Savior through Jesus Christ our Lord. All glory, majesty, power, and authority are his before all time, and in the present, and beyond all time! Amen.

### Consider This

One night during our bedtime routine one of my daughters said, "Daddy, sing the Ology song."

"Did you say the theology song?" I asked.

"No! The OLOGY song!"

After a bit of back and forth like this, I finally figured it out when she said, "The song when we give the money."

She wanted the Doxology, the one we sing every Sunday in worship after the offering:

Praise God, from Whom all blessings flow;
Praise Him, all creatures here below;
Praise Him above, ye heavenly host;
Praise Father, Son, and Holy Ghost. Amen.

A doxology is a hymn of praise to the Trinity. We sing this at our church as the offering of the congregation's tithes and gifts are placed on the altar as a public recognition that everything we have comes from God. And now it's also what we sing at bedtime to end our day as a family.

"Doxology" is rooted in the Greek word *doxa* which means "glory," but also means "of the nature and acts of God."

So a doxology is about the "glory of God." And the glory of God is the character, nature, and revelation of God found in the relationship and actions between the Father, Son, and Holy Spirit.

As Jude wraps up his warnings about false teachings and his call to defend the faith, he doesn't sign off in the usual way letters were finished back then. Instead, he offers a doxology:

> Now all glory to God, who is able to keep you from falling away and will bring you with great joy into his

glorious presence without a single fault. All glory to
him who alone is God, our Savior through Jesus Christ
our Lord. All glory, majesty, power, and authority are
his before all time, and in the present, and beyond all
time! Amen. (vv. 24–25)

This is far from a nice little bow to tie up his letter. This
is the big finale, and it offers us a piece of a formula for
defending the faith that J. D. Walt taught me in seminary:

Theology – Doxology = Ideology

Theology is the study of God and religious doctrine. It's
what we learn and know about God. But doxology goes
beyond knowledge to adoration. It is the acknowledgment of
who God is because of a relationship. And you must have the
two together. I can know everything about my wife, but if
we don't have a relationship of love and respect, then things
don't go well.

So then if we have theology (what we know about God)
without doxology (a relationship of love and respect with
God) we end up with ideology: the opinions and ideas of individuals or groups. And ideologies can be slippery. Everyone
has an opinion, and they can shift with changes in culture
and experience. They can become a source of . . . wait for it
. . . false teaching and the false self.

Which leads us to another formula based on all we've seen
in Jude:

False Self + False Teaching = False Gods

And what is a false god? An idol. And idolatry is the worship and adoration of someone or something else as God. Idolatry puts each of us right back in the garden of Eden—right next to Adam and Eve—putting our trust in something and someone else other than God.

And that is a formula for being false. It's why Jude ends his theology letter with a doxology. Because as J. D. also formulated:

Theology + Doxology = Reality

And that's the truth.

### The Prayer

Jesus, give me more and more mercy, peace, and love. That's the formula for today, and that's enough. Amen.

### The Question

• What is your formula?

# 44 To Be Continued

**JUDE 25B | Amen.**

### Consider This

"Amen" is the signal that we're done. The most common modern definition is "so be it." It usually serves as the prayer version of "The End." Jude ends his letter with "amen" and we move on. But what if that's not really the end?

The word *amen* originates in the Old Testament Hebrew meaning "truth." To put it in more practical terms, to say "amen" at the end of a prayer or a sermon means something like, "What you've said is the truth."

Second Corinthians 1:20 says, "For no matter how many promises God has made, they are 'Yes' in Christ. And so through him the 'Amen' is spoken by us to the glory of God" (NIV). In other words, through Jesus the truth is spoken by you and me. With that in mind, consider the pattern these last three days on how to defend the faith against false teaching. Jude begins with you and me individually:

> But you, dear friends, must build each other up in your most holy faith, pray in the power of the Holy Spirit, and await the mercy of our Lord Jesus Christ, who will bring you eternal life. In this way, you will keep yourselves safe in God's love. (vv. 20–21)

Then he moves to how we deal with others:

> And you must show mercy to those whose faith is wavering. Rescue others by snatching them from the flames of judgment. Show mercy to still others, but do so with great caution, hating the sins that contaminate their lives. (vv. 22–23)

Then he concludes with God's actions and nature:

> Now all glory to God, who is able to keep you from falling away and will bring you with great joy into his glorious presence without a single fault. All glory to

> him who alone is God, our Savior through Jesus Christ
> our Lord. All glory, majesty, power, and authority are
> his before all time, and in the present, and beyond all
> time! Amen. (vv. 24–25)

Distill it down to its most basic form and we get *you for the sake of others because of God.*

This is the amen, the truth we speak with our lives. It's an amen defended by loving the Lord with all our heart, soul, and mind and loving our neighbor as ourselves, which is the pattern if you reverse the order of Jude's ending. See what he did there?

And so Jude ends his letter on defending against what is false with an amen that is not a "the end" but a "to be continued" until Jesus returns. Can I get an amen?

### The Prayer
Jesus, give me more and more mercy, peace, and love. Amen and amen.

### The Question
- What was the most challenging word for you from Jude?

# Thank-You Notes

When I graduated high school, family and friends sent me gifts, and my mother demanded I write thank-you cards. I didn't want to, but she said if I didn't then they wouldn't give me gifts when I graduated college (or got married or had kids). So I reluctantly hand-wrote the notes.

I've since learned the real gift is not what they gave me but thankfulness itself. Pen to paper in my own bad handwriting is the sign between you and me that we are not doing this alone, and for that I am thankful. So then:

**Thank you** to my wife, Jennifer, and my daughters, Sadie, Norah, and Lilly. Because these Daily Text posts were literally written and posted daily, it meant I was writing and recording during and after bedtime. I am thankful you believe in my call to write and the mission of the Daily Text to take this on as a family, even if it meant missing a few dinners and bedtime songs.

**Thank you** to J. D. Walt for again trusting me with substitute writing for the Daily Text. You taught me that "a writer writes" and "great is the enemy of good enough," which is the wisdom that gets the Daily Text posted daily.

**Thank you** to Drew Causey for taking the time to talk with me through some of these hard passages. I could not have navigated this without you, and I'm thankful for your willingness and friendship.

**Thank you** to Micah Smith for walking with me through the minefield of some of this material and helping me "make the donuts." You still write the best thank-you notes ever.

**Thank you** to Andy Miller, Holly Jones, Andrew Dragos, and Nick Perreault for your work making this happen, and thank you to the rest of the Seedbed Farm Team. All y'all are champions for Jesus.

**Thank you** to the Daily Text Nation for not just reading but also *interacting* with what we're sowing here. It's not always easy, but Jesus is good, and I'm thankful to sow for a great awakening with you.

CPSIA information can be obtained
at www.ICGtesting.com
Printed in the USA
LVHW031602061219
639668LV00006B/10/P

9 781628 247435